SPIDDAL ROAD

by

Anna Pearce

ISBN-13: 978-1500381868
ISBN-10: 1500381861

'When the student is ready the teacher appears'.
Along this incredible journey there were many lessons;
Some harder to grasp than others:
I learnt tolerance from the intolerant,
Found strength when I thought all was lost,
I was shown kindness from complete strangers
And in my darkest hour I found my 'thin place'.

The Driving force behind this story, was born of a promise made.

I dedicate this book to my mother.

Chapter One

Deep in thought, Annie Quinn stood in the car park of Wattle Ridge Nursing Home. With her back towards the large red brick building, she commanded a panoramic view out over the shimmering lights of a world that had brought her to this moment in time. There was a sickening panic in her stomach. 'Run,' it said; 'run as far away from here as you can.' Another voice taunted, with a thousand reasons, why she should stay.

Her first shift in the Dementia ward had hit hard. It wasn't the work itself, but the all consuming sadness that seemed to whisper its melancholy from the very walls inside Wattle Ridge. 'I'll talk to Greg,' she told herself, 'he'll understand. And tomorrow I'll ring reception and simply tell them, it was not what I had expected.'

Greg was asleep when she arrived home. She made a decision not to disturb him; instead, taking a pillow and blanket, she lay out in front of the fire. She watched as the flames threw shadows onto the walls. Faces of old people filled her imagery. 'Please, I want to go home,' each would ask, while showing the same sad and lost countenance. She felt that each of these souls had judged her, and having done so, had placed an irrational, yet, almost tangible blame on her, for their circumstances. In another time, these men and women had been contributing, lucid and healthy individuals; lovers, teachers, fishermen, engineers, students, fathers and mothers, each armed with their own unique dreams and aspirations. But like the flames of the fire, they too had spent the full thrust of life's energy, to the point where they also had been reduced to fading embers, destined to linger in a world that had reduced them to wander aimlessly through the pallid halls of the nursing home.

A realisation dawned on Annie, that this was the same fate awaiting her own mother, Kate. Kate, lived on the other side of the world, and had been diagnosed with Alzheimer's disease. The thought of this dreaded disease sent a shiver of horror through Annie's spine. 'What if my mother lived in that place?' she thought. 'What would I want for her? There could only be the one answer. She decided there and then that she would stick with the job and would do everything in her power to enhance the quality of life for all the residents placed in her care. 'Perhaps,' she thought, 'my efforts, like the flutter of a butterfly wing, may reach all the way across the seas and have a profound effect on my mother's carers in Ireland.'

In her previous job, Annie had cared for people in their own homes. But in Wattle Ridge, she now worked in a team situation and she was enjoying the added social interaction.

She silently watched one evening while an otherwise stoic and matronly nurse lovingly stroked the face of a dying woman. The nurse had prepared the room with soft lighting and music. Annie felt she would be so happy if her own mother received this same loving care. There were some in the profession who were cold, and sometimes rough, with the residents. It could simply be a harsh tone, or a rough hand. When she witnessed this behaviour she would try to linger until *nurse nasty* had left, and then give the resident a touch on the cheek, a smile, often a caring word to balance the *nasty.*

Dementia was to be Annie's calling. "You have a full stop on your face," one resident said, as she bent to help her undress. The woman pointed to a mole on Annie's face and repeated, "You have a full stop on your face." In her prime, the old woman had been a schoolteacher.

On another occasion, Annie noticed a woman with what appeared to be the world's biggest smile. The woman had found someone else's false teeth and put them in her mouth along with her own.

The Priest, who came to the Nursing Home, told Annie, that it was ok to see the funny side of dementia, 'It helps to keep ones spirits up,' he had said, adding that his own grandmother had this disease and her behaviour often made him smile. They exchanged stories: 'A dear lady I used to visit,' he continued, 'was showing serious signs of memory loss. The doctor had diagnosed her with dementia, and when she tried to recall his diagnosis for me, she said, The doctor told me I have dem-dem-dem Domestos.'

It was while working at Wattle Ridge that Annie came face to face with mortality. A sweet old woman had died while she was bathing her. The experience for Annie, though sad, felt surprisingly spiritual and peaceful. Annie felt it an honour to be with her at such a special time.

Chapter Two

As a child growing up in Ballyfermot, Annie spent most of her summer hours collecting bees, in jam jars. She would bring them home and study their bodies; she loved their fine gossamer wings. She marvelled at the different species she caught, and it gave her great joy to see them tucked safely inside their own special universe, a universe that she had created, God-like, just for them. However, she never kept them too long and always let them go. The bees became a warm part of her childhood memories. She never lost her fondness for these beautiful creatures.

Ballyfermot, *'the largest housing estate in Europe'*. How proud Annie was to be part of something so monumental. She was a romantic dreamer, with an imagination that buzzed liked her bees. A polite and attentive child in school, she often lost herself in the history and mythology of what she called, her *'beautiful Ireland.'* It was not surprising therefore, that while at school, she fell in love with the poems of William Butler Yeats, the *lake Isle of Innisfree,* being her favourite, and in particular the line which read, *'and I shall have some peace there'*. This line became ingrained in her psyche. She would often try to imagine a place where everyone was at peace.

Oliver, her father had been banging, sawing and painting, for what seemed like days, when all of a sudden a wall appeared and it changed their two-bedroom corporation house into three. Annie now shared a room with her sister, Theresa, while her younger siblings, Anthony and Thomas, shared the adjoining room. This period of Annie's life was largely carefree and happy; however, she would recall feeling slightly disturbed by the sound, the key made, in the front door lock, when Oliver came home from the pub. She loved her father dearly yet, she understood certain feelings, not as *fear,* but rather *confusion.* She was never sure if she should make eye contact with him, as he stood and swayed in the centre of the room. She felt whatever choice she made, it would be wrong.

Each weekday on Spiddal Road, came with its own particular meal: Mondays, was Sundays left over's, Tuesday stew, Wednesday potatoes, egg and beans, Thursday more stew and Friday chips. Annie was never hungry, yet, she was conscious of her mother's amazing skill at putting a hot meal together. It seems so long ago now, as she reaches out to touch, smell and taste those memories.

Annie enjoyed her mother's company, and recalls sitting on a stool in the kitchen, dressed in a favourite, light blue pleated, dress that showed her skinny legs dangling inches above the linoleum. In her memory, she's licking the cake mix from a wooden spoon.

She often watched as her mother garnered food items from the larder: a packet of tea, sugar, bread, biscuits and sometimes a slab of real butter, cut from the block. All these items and more would then be carefully placed in a shopping bag. Kate, aware that her child was watching, would turn and say, "always remember sweetheart, *you can share a crumb with a bird.*" She would then ask, as if it were for the very first time, "would you like to come go to the city with me Annie?" The excitement of the moment never failed. Annie would jump down from the kitchen chair and stand up, straight as a soldier, while her mother buttoned up her thick winter coat.

Pressing her face against the upstairs window on the bus, she felt the tingling expectation of the approaching vibrant city of Dublin. The streetlights, during those dim smog filled days, became fireworks, as they sped past the bus window. Her mother sensing Annie's excitement would lean across and wipe the condensation from the glass with her coat sleeve.

Arriving near the tenements, Annie held her mother's hand while they walked, through the rain, towards the old buildings. Climbing two flights of concrete stairs, and after passing several identical windows and doors, they reached their destination. A tiny grey haired woman, beaming the warmest smile, answered their knock. "Kate, how lovely," she greeted. "I see you've brought your sweet Annie to lighten up my home," she added, while stooping to tenderly touch Annie's face. Annie watched as Kate then spread out the banquet of food on the kitchen table. The woman gasped, her hand covered her mouth and her eyes grew larger with astonishment. It was at that very moment that Annie realised that she was a part of something special.

"Sure, it's nothing," offered Kate, "Just a few morsels."

Little Mo was Annie's nickname at school. She was aware that she was small, but was none the less, comfortable with her stature; the exception being, when she stood waiting for the annual Girl Guide's photograph to be taken. Feeling that her belt and stocking were too big and didn't hang right, and while desperately wanting to look her best for the shutter, she snuck a hand behind her back, pulled the belt tight like a tourniquet, to make a hopeful adjustment to her wardrobe, and smiled cheekily at the camera. Simple things, such as pretty hairclips and the silver foil from the Easter eggs brought her joy. Sometimes her father would buy her pictures of Saints, from the church kiosk. Annie considered it her holy duty to keep these pictures safe, and would place them between the pages of her small prayer book. She often wondered why, in the pictures, the Saints looked so serious and burdensome.

She recalls the teacher introducing a new girl to the class and asking, 'who wants to be Clara's friend?' Annie raised her hand and started a friendship that lasted for decades.

As a ten year old, Annie remembers sitting at her father's feet while watching telly. Around this time there were ongoing industrial actions with the coal miners in England. She watched as her dad interacted with the television, 'fair play to ye lads,' he'd say, and 'don't let them bastards rip you off.' Annie became so influenced by his words, that when the teacher announced the cancellation of a double period of gym, adding that it would be substituted with geography, she became so incensed at the change of routine that she called together a small band of classmates. They all agreed they were being ripped off.

"The hall is rightfully ours every Tues afternoon girls," she proclaimed, as she incited her comrades to tear a page from their copy books and write the words, 'STRIKE ON HERE'.

When her teacher returned from her break, Annie called out, "ok girls!' On this signal, the Gang of Five, led by Annie, approached the teacher's desk, where they marched in a tight circle while chanting, 'strike on here, strike on here.' A note was sent home with Annie, but she can't recall, what, if anything came of the industrial action.

Later that year her teacher introduced a student teacher, Miss Clarke, to the class. As part of Miss Clarke's training, she was to shadow the regular teacher. At the end of her first two weeks, Miss Clarke was required to choose a student to be the subject of an essay. She chose Annie. The school contacted Annie's parents for their permission and, much to Annie's delight, they agreed. Annie got a bit carried away by the whole thing. She thought she was going to become a movie star and Miss Clarke got an invite to Annie's house for tea.

Holding her hand, Annie walked Miss Clarke the long way home, so as to show her off. She wanted to shout out to the whole of Ballyfermot, 'Look everybody? This is Miss Clarke. She's going to write a movie about me.' Annie's parents made Miss Clarke very welcome and while they talked, Annie drooled over the chocolate biscuits that had been bought for the occasion. When Annie was finally invited, by her mother, to have a biscuit, she waited a polite moment, and then picked up one of the chocolate goldgrain biscuits, between finger and thumb, and making an attempt to look sophisticated, she stuck out her little pinkie.

Neither the book 'nor the movie ever eventuated but Annie grew up with two new words in her vocabulary: Naivety and humility.

Some time later, her brother, Anthony, was chosen from his school, to appear in a children's television show called TRIPLE TROPLE. Anthony was a fun lad, so Annie understood why they picked him. Again their parents, Kate and Oliver, received a letter explaining that someone from the telly would be calling on them. The excitement mounted. 'Anthony Murray's going to be on the telly'. Sure the whole street was talking. Then one evening the knock finally came. A good looking well dressed man, stood at the front door, "Are you Mrs. Kate Murray?" he asked.

"I am," said Kate. "Are you here about the telly?"

"I am," the man smiled.

"Come in, mister," she said, "and I'll stick the kettle on." The man's face lit up. It was a bitter cold evening, and Kate said to him, "Don't be shy. Go get yourself warm by the fire." She then called up the stairs. "Anthony, the man from the telly's here." Anthony dashed down and Kate began grooming him, while insisting he be polite to the telly man. Kate left the room for a few minutes and returned with a tray containing tea and cake. The telly man looked amazed.

"Thanks very much Mrs. Murray, this is very kind of you. I don't normally receive such wonderful treatment."

"Really," said Kate. "Sure, I would have imagined, with your job, people would be delighted to see you?"

"Absolutely not, Mrs Murray. Which brings me to the matter

in hand. According to our records, you have not paid your television licence." Kate nearly fell out of her standing. The gentleman himself showed much sympathy, to Kate's embarrassment, and gave her an extension to pay the bill.

Soon afterwards, Anthony did actually appear on Triple Trople, and in front of the entire population of Ireland, he ran straight *alongside of*, instead of, *in and out of*, the hurdles to claim the prize. Kate and her family sat in front of the telly and laughed till they cried.

Chapter Three

As a teenager Annie was the first home from work. She would like to sit in the kitchen and keep her mother company, while she prepared the family dinner. Stew was a favourite for Annie and on the cold winter nights it never failed to hit the spot. She recalls her sister Theresa coming into the kitchen one time, and after taking a look at the stew, she declared, "I am not eating that shit!" Kate's reaction was to apologise, and make her sausage and chips instead. Kate actually set the meal on a tray and served it to her, in front of the fire. A fleeting thought struck Annie, that her mother might have favoured her older sister. Annie preferred to be with her mum in the kitchen, and such thoughts she chose to simply brush off.

In later years, Annie would watch Kate wrap a hot dinner in foil, place it in the basket of her bicycle, and cycle it across Ballyfermot to her own aging mother, Aggie. Annie's grandmother, Aggie, had Alzheimer's disease. It was the first time that Annie had heard the word Alzheimer's. Kate and her brother took turns in staying with Aggie. But as the disease progressed, Aggie developed constant health problems. She had a tendency to walk away from the house in total confusion, day and night. Despite the family's best efforts it proved impossible to keep her at home. After an emotional family meeting, inspired by advice from the district nurse, the family agreed that it would be for the best to place Aggie in a nursing home. However, the family were simply devastated. Annie's teary eyed visit to the nursing home, for the first time, culminated with one of the nurses putting an arm around her. The nurse explained that, emotionally, Alzheimer's was far worse for the family members than it was for the person with the disease. She went on to reassure Annie that her grandmother was in the right place.

Annie was at this stage married to Damien and she had given birth to two healthy children, Lisa and Daithi. As a family, they had applied to emigrate to Australia. It would take almost two years before their application was accepted, by which time, Annie had acquired, if not cold feet, then certainly conflicting thoughts on leaving her family. She explained her dilemma to the Australian embassy and received a couple of month's grace, in order to make a final decision.

During this period she would visit her grandmother two or three times a week. She had noticed during these visits that the old people, in the nursing home, enjoyed the company of her children. It appeared to lift their spirits and the experience was a great lesson for the little ones in accepting the frailty of the aged. Annie had learned this lesson from her own mother, and was happy to pass it on.

After one of these visits Annie called at her sister's house. Accompanying her were, her two children, and her daughters five years old friend, Wan Yee.

While Annie's sister Theresa was making a cup of tea, Annie took Wan Yee by the hand and led her into the parlour to show her the tropical fish in the aquarium. Wan Yee had never seen the likes of such a spectacle and began jumping and clapping with joy. Her innocence made Annie smile. After Annie returned to her own home, Theresa rang her and they engaged in small talk. Just after Annie hung up the phone, she realized that she had forgotten to mention something, and picked up the receiver. To her surprise she could hear Theresa talking. Theresa had somehow left the line open, and Annie was listening to her talking with her husband Adrian. *"And you'll never guess,"* she heard her say. *"Annie just took Wan Yee into the front parlour, as brazen as you like, and showed her your fish. Who the fuck does she think she is?"* Annie's mouth fell open, as she over-heard her sister continue to deride her to Adrian. Theresa's tone was loaded with so much malice that, by the end of it, Annie was in a state of shock. The last words she heard from Theresa was, *"I'm going next door for a while."*

Annie immediately jumped into her car, and drove the five minute journey to her sister's house. Adrian answered the door. "She's popped next door," he said.

"I know!" said Annie, still shaking. "Will you tell her, I heard every nasty word she said about me? And by the way Adrian, your phone is off the hook!"

Later that evening, Theresa phoned Annie, *"I believe you called,"* she said, curtly.

"Yes," Annie replied. "I am so upset at what I heard."

"I've been meaning to talk to you about 'things' for a while," said Theresa.

"About what?"

"All sorts of things! Every time I ring your house, your children are outside playing. "

"And your point is?"

"Your children are never in the house with you."

"My children are happy, whether they are inside or out," Annie replied. "I simply don't get your point." Theresa's criticisms went on to included, Annie not taking her children to mass, and continued with such a vindictive tone that by the end of their conversation   Annie   was   completely distraught.

Sometime during the next few days Annie rang the Australian Embassy and agreed to finalise the paperwork for emigration. Having committed, meant doing a lot of things in a short space of time. The house went on the market and sold quicker than expected; leaving a rush to sell the contents. This part of the plan fell into place with only two exceptions: The Christmas tree. Kate had bought it for Annie, from the Woolworths store where she worked. It had been the stores display tree and now it held pride of place in Annie's sitting room. 'It's a fine tree,' Annie had said, in a futile bid to convince Damien to bring it to Australia. The second item, causing an arm wrestle, was a huge red toy tractor which Daithi their son owned.

Daithi, at four years old became a 'mascot' for the teenagers on the street. They would knock on Annie's door asking if he could hang out with them. These older kids carried him up and down the street on their shoulders. Looking out the window, Annie once saw them throwing him from person to person, causing him to scream with delight. She knew the teenagers loved Daithi, and he loved hanging out with them. When he was not being a mascot, he would be inseparable from his big red tractor. Annie had tried Damien's patience by suggestion that there might be room to take the tractor to Australia.

The contents sale had begun, and Annie felt uneasy as her pictures, toaster, crockery, and cutlery started to walk out the front door in the arms of strangers.

With the departure date approaching, they decided to spend the last week with Annie's parents in Ballyfermot. There would be no big party or great fuss made of the upcoming auspicious occasion. Annie simply got a few friends together, for a coffee in Ballyfermot. She did feel the knot in her stomach begin to tighten as she fare-welled her friends.

Earlier that week, Oliver had announced, that neither he nor Kate would be going to Dublin airport for the send off. 'The sadness,' he had told Annie, 'would be more than he could bear.'

The moment had arrived. Annie threw her arms around her dad and wept. He pushed her away slightly, but she knew it was because his heart was breaking. Turning she looked into her mother's eyes, and the hardest farewell had suddenly become so much harder. Her chest ached as she forced herself out through the front door and along the garden path.

While Damien helped the driver, with the children and the cases, Annie stopped at the gate, and turned. The net curtains were pulled to one side and she could see Oliver, he was standing in full view, with the palm of his hand placed flat, in a sign of love, on the inside of the pane of glass. Beside him, Kate's melancholic countenance, struggled to maintain a heart-broken smile. Annie's lips trembled as she mouthed to her parents, 'I love you so much.' She then turned and, without another look, she sped away.

It was December 1989 when they arrived in Australia. At that time her parents were in good health, but Aggie would die a short time later. Annie took comfort in the fact that Kate was at her mother's side for the last three days of her life.

The fresh start in Australia became something of a paradox for Annie. She loved the new experiences and adventures that her new start offered. However, she missed her kin folk and her homeland. There was a shortage of electricians at the time in Australia and Damien quickly found employment. Lisa and Daithi enrolled in the local school, but would not start until after the Christmas break. Annie dreaded that first school day. She had begun to struggle with homesickness. The school year didn't begin until the first of February, so she enjoyed having her little ones around her a while longer. When the first school day arrived, and while amongst all the parents at assembly, Annie knelt down and wept, as her two children hugged her goodbye.

When she returned to pick them up, Daithi's teacher spoke with her. "Daithi is a wonderful child," she said. "I asked him how he was doing, and he replied, grand! Such a big word, to come from the mouth of such a little boy. And such a charming accent."

Annie fondly remembers the first day the family went for an adventure into Sydney. The train pulled into Circular Quay and on seeing the opera house, Daithi loudly exclaimed, "Mammy, look at... look at... the leaning Tower of Pisa!" With this the whole carriage erupted into laughter.

Chapter Four

The following year Annie's parents came to Australia for a holiday. Ever since Annie could remember, her father, had held a conviction that one day, someone would try to break into his home, or as he called it, his 'castle.' Each time the family left the house, he would insist on the same bizarre ceremony. The two girls would leave first and go up the road, minutes later the boys would leave and go down the road, lastly both parents would leave, and they would all meet up around the corner. It was crazy behaviour. Oliver became so anxious about the security of his castle that he cut his trip to Australia short and returned to Ireland. Kate remained with Annie for a further five months and enjoyed the time of her life.

During her stay in Australia, Kate got involved with an 'outreach' program that supported people suffering from Alzheimer's disease, and Annie joined her, twice a week. Working alongside her mother proved special for Annie. As volunteers they took people for outings on buses or stayed in the centre and sang songs with them. Annie and her mother shared long conversations about Alzheimer's, including its debilitating affects. Kate confided to Annie that her greatest fear was, that she might one day succumb to this disease. Annie responded with a *promise* to take care of her, if that ever did happen. "Mam, I will come home! I promise that I will be there for you." They hugged. "You are the best mum," she said, "and you don't ever need to worry about such matters."

When Kate returned to Ireland, she continued her voluntary work. She had come to the realisation that carer's needed respite from their tireless job. The local health centre in Ballyfermot was helpful to Kate, by locating for her a community hall. A man named Tom, kindly offered his services as the bus driver. Tuesday was the day chosen.

Kate worked for many years running her one day a week care

centre. Many people on the Ballyfermot estate looked forward to Tuesdays, and for some it was the only help they got.

In Australia, Annie kept herself busy with a school reading group. The children would listen intently to the words she spoke. It wasn't the story that was intriguing them; it was her broad Irish accent. She smiled as she watched their open mouths; their concentration taking in every syllable she uttered. But there was a melancholy dogging her, and she had a daily struggle to shake it off. She suspected it was not homesickness but something deeper, something from her childhood. There were demons and somehow they had clambered into her suitcase and migrated with her.

After reading an article, and making a few enquiries, she joined a group called Al Anon. Al Anon had been established to help people, who had been affected, usually, by a family member's alcohol abuse.

One sunny spring morning she found herself in a small room with a handful of women. After listening nervously, while each spoke of the affect that alcohol had had on them, she was then asked, if she would care to share her story. This simple invitation was the beginning of an understanding of her childhood, in particular, the affect her father's alcoholism had on her life. She came to understand her father's pain and ultimately to forgive him. That auspicious moment, for Annie, when a complete stranger invited her, to share her story, eventually led her to sing Al Anon's praises, and to become the secretary of their local branch. Al Anon, as with AA, uses a twelve step program. Annie found this to be a powerful 'life tool.'

Around this time, she won a part time position working for a welfare agency. Her role was to look after children while their mothers received counselling. Annie endeared herself to many of her peers there, and consequently, several friendships were formed.

One day she received permission to sit in on a counselling session. It was entitled 'the child within'. The facilitator brought the women, through meditation, to a series of visualizations. They were, at the climax, to meet the small child (which was you) and having done so, to bend down and hug her. Annie obviously took this session very serious, because when it got to the latter part, she wept uncontrollably. Later that night she put pen to paper and wrote:

Annie Quinn.
Who is this child in a blue pleated dress?
With her shiny dark hair, and her shoes in a mess
I've been watching her now, and I feel a bit puzzled
As I journey this road, which is fairly less travelled
She's a sweet darling child, with a heart made of gold
Who loves to catch bees not for merit or scold
For the bees are her friend, and never a foe
She will keep them a while, and then let them all go

She plays in the daisies, but cries in her bed
For the things that she heard, were all better unsaid
She carries the hurt, the guilt, and the shame
While telling herself, 'never ever again'

If love brings this pain, then she'd rather not know
Just undo the lid, and let them all go
Like the bees in her jar, through the glass that looked fine
Her freedom's enthralled by a transparent line

Ah! This poor little child who struggles to view
A world that is happy contented and true
I ventured to hold her and banish her pain
I ventured to teach her to dance once again

Her face was familiar, her eyes were so clear
Her heart beat a rhythm both of love and of fear
I asked her to trust me to let me come in
I am you; I sang softly, we are both Annie Quinn

Annie found it both interesting and sad that her father didn't talk to her for quite a long time after reading her poem. '*She played in the daisies, but cried in her bed*', maybe it was that line? However, since she found Al Anon, she began to 'get it.'

Annie's mother, Kate, was diagnosed with Alzheimer's disease in early 2001. Later that same year Annie's father died. Annie was saddened at his death, but she had not learned to hate him, as some had. She felt sorry that he was not as well loved as he could have been. 'How on earth could a bollix like Ollie, have produced such a lovely girl as yourself,' was a comment from a co-worker to Annie. Oliver had secured Annie's first job in the canteen where he worked. She became known as the '*sweetheart of Chloride Ireland*,' and her father, Oliver was known as the '*bollix*.' But he was her Dad, and that fact would never change.

Oliver would have been proud of the turnout for his funeral. Thomas, Annie's brother, and now a sailor, had organised a mini bus full of uniformed comrades from Cork to form a guard around the church. The service was poignant, with lots of participation from Oliver's children and grandchildren. Annie read a eulogy. She wrote it while travelling from Australia. '*He may not pull through*,' they had said.

Annie began her eulogy.
"*Last Friday, at my home in Australia, I received the phone call that we all dread. HE MAY NOT PULL THROUGH! The caller said. So, with family support and a lot of things falling into place, both Daithi and I got the chance to come home. I just needed to hold my dad's warm hand. The hand that picked me up as a child when I fell over, the hand that showed me discipline when I needed to be brought into line, the hand that would write long and detailed letters informing me of all the news back home, and that same hand that would pick up the phone and ring for a chat that always ended with him saying 'I love you'.*

"*HE MAY NOT PULL THROUGH" In order to relieve my pain, I*

tried to dwell on the negatives. It didn't work. I have come to realise that the love I hold for my father, my mother and my family, is stored in a special place, a safe place.   I selfishly I wanted my dad to stay alive. When I arrived in Dublin, I was scared of being told that my fears were a reality. However, I did get to hold Dads warm hand. He was in a coma, yet he sent me a tear, which tumbled down his cheek. I prayed I prayed hard to the God of my understanding, to help him. The adult part of me began to prepare, while the child part of me was hoping against hope that he would pull through.

While in transit, in Japan, I began to write down my happy memories: Beautiful summer trips to Dollymount Strand and Sandymount, bucket, spades and ham sandwiches. The sand always got in between the slices of bread. But we didn't care.

On Christmas Eve my parents would allow the reindeers into the kitchen. We all knew the reindeers had been, because we saw their muddy paw prints and the half eaten carrots strewn across the floor. I smile with appreciation for my parents allowing the reindeers to dirty the kitchen floor, just for us.

The paws prints actually belonged to our dog lassie. I remember so clearly dad announcing that lassie needed to go to the pound, because she was having too many puppies. We thought that the puppies were wonderful. Anthony's singing career began in the back yard singing to the puppies.

I was with dad when he took Lassie on the bus into Dublin City. Her eyes held an idea of his intention. She stared up at me the whole journey. When I burst into tears, Dad melted and brought her back home to go on as before doing her reindeer impressions, with her paw prints on our kitchen floor.

Dad I have managed the odd smile over the past few days. On seeing you doing the gorilla walk, after Greg did his party piece, that always brings a smile. We all laughed so much that night.

    My friends in Australia send their love to you Dad. You taught me the value of honesty and the importance of integrity.

'Sweetheart,' you would say, *'there is no amount of riches, fancy cars, or worldly possessions that mean more than integrity. It's all that we have; it's the only thing worth fighting for.'* I thank you for that lesson Dad. To me you were a great man. I miss you already and I will always love you. It is now time to bid you farewell on your journey. Watch over us dad. Enjoy the coming of your new grandchild; a testament that tomorrow the sun will rise and give us a new day.

I am very proud to say that I, Annie Quinn, am the second child of Oliver Murray."

After the service, the cortège stopped, for one minute, outside Oliver's house on Spiddal Road, for Oliver's final *'Going Home'*. From the mourning car, Annie watched two little boys who, only a second earlier had been playing on the street, stood perfectly still and bowed their heads in respect. The scene was bitter sweet.

During the wake, she listened to her uncle speak of the time he and Oliver sat side by side on bar stools. The uncle spoke of how the usually stoic Oliver became teary eyed, while confessing that he loved and missed his Annie in Australia.

A voice called to Annie from outside the doorway of the wake, "Annie, come here? I have something for you." It was her cousin, Liam. "This is for you," he said, handing her a, green cast metal, model of a Dublin bus. "Do you remember what this is about?" he asked. She smiled.

"Yes Liam." They both laughed. "I'm sorry," she said, maintaining her smile, "I didn't mean to get you into trouble."

As a young girl, she had been travelling with her dad on the bus when a pair of hands appeared on the outside of the window beside her. Then a head popped up to reveal it was Liam. Annie made a frown of disapproval and he let go and *popped off*. A few days later whilst visiting her aunt, she piped up, "Your Liam was scutting the bus the other day." ('Scutting' was a dare-devil way that the kids on the estate would escape the bus fare by hanging onto the side of the bus.)

When Liam came home that evening his mother slapped the back of his head and said, "Scutting the bus were you? So that's where you got your injuries; not playing soccer, eh." Annie had a soft spot for Liam.

After Oliver's funeral, all Kate's children accompanied her home to Spiddal Road. They each opened a personal letter that Oliver had written, including one for Kate. His intent was for the letters to be read after his death. The letters had been placed five years prior, in a large brown envelope, along with written instructions for them to be opened on the day of his funeral. Silently each member of the family read their personal letter. Tears tumbled down Annie's face as she read hers.

April 13, 1996

This letter is to you Annie, and as I told Thomas, Theresa, and Anthony, there is no reply required. The fact that I am not around will tell you that.

There are no words to let you know how much I love you, as I love your sister and brothers.
You were always the gigglier, the little girl always full of laughs, and the funny one. You were the peg girl.
When I got to work, it was nothing to find about 6 pegs hanging from my coat. My, they were happy days.

Here I am on Saturday morning, April 13 at 7.30am, thinking of you half way around the world. Just to pour out some of my feelings to you and let you know, how I love you and miss seeing you.

I hope to be around for midnight of the month of December, in the year 2000, to see in a new year, a new century, and the big one, the new millennium. Please God.

My hope for you is that you are happy in what you do and don't forget to remember me to your new partner and the three children.

Used to love visiting you in Tallaght with your two lovely

children, Lisa and Daithi. I enjoyed my stay with you in Australia.
God knows I may do once again.

I'll always remember the time you fell down the stairs, not
once but twice. The funny thing, about those events, you just upped
and walked away. The other two events were, when the house
flooded twice because of your nose bleeds.

After all those things you're still a little 'Pet', and always go
on being one. Don't ever forget me, and always spare a prayer for
me. I am certain we will meet again. I've told mam that I will be
waiting inside The Gate; sure I might as well wait there for you

I love you Annie, and always have.
You're a little dear, love you

Dad xxx

Twelve days, was all the time Annie had in Ireland. She felt she wanted to be as helpful as possible to her family during this time. What to do with Oliver's clothes?' was a touchy subject for the family. However, they reached a consensus that it would be better for Kate, not to have to see Oliver's things hanging there. Everyone was pleased when Kate decided to give everything to charity.

A week after the funeral Annie prepared herself for the deed. Armed with black plastic bags she went into her parent's bedroom. 'Sorry dad, it's for mam's sake that I do this,' she whispered to herself.

Oliver always kept his belongings, hung or stacked neatly, in their respective places. There was a necktie for every conceivable occasion. Annie looked at these one by one, and marvelled at some in particular before respectfully placing all his clothing in the five bags.

Something caught her eye. The paper lining on the uppermost shelf was raised. Lifting the paper revealed a letter. She recognised Oliver's handwriting. She had always admired how artistic his written words were. The letter was addressed, *to the finder,* 'that's me,' she thought and with some apprehension, she opened it.

Scanning through the many foolscap pages, she realised that it was a lengthy poem. She sat on the bed and carefully read Oliver's account of life. She was shocked when she read of his betrayal. *The worst betrayal to befall any child.* Like most victims of child abuse Oliver had silently carried his secret all this time for fear of having to relive the pain. His letter concluded by asking forgiveness for any hurt that he had brought to his family. He also asked, that the finder deal with the written information as they see fit. Annie sat for what seemed like an age. Then while Kate was busy in the kitchen, Annie folded the letter, brought it down stairs, and burnt it.

Months later in Australia, she confided, what she had read, to her doctor. He strongly advised her against harbouring this secret, stating that it would be far better to reveal it to her siblings and to her mother. Annie took his advice, with the exception of her mother.

Chapter Five

On a trip back to Ireland in 2008, she was shocked to see how much her mother's living conditions had deteriorated. A large block of ice had formed around the freezer box and was stopping the fridge door from closing. Someone, presumably Kate, had placed newspapers and old rags on the floor in an attempt to absorb the constant dripping from the ice block. The result was that the rags had become slimy and dank. It had been eight years since Oliver had died, and it was obvious that Kate couldn't cope. It was also obvious that the fireplace had not been used in a long time and with no other heating source in the house, Kate must have struggled to keep warm. Annie imagined Kate living alone for eight years without heat, and how she must have suffered.

She found dozens of electricity bills, all showing, 'in credit.' pensioners in Ireland are given free units, and Kate's units, for whatever reason, had not been used. Surely whoever payed her bills, must have seen this? The bed was filthy beyond description, and there were thousands of Euros' stuffed inside a pillowcase. When asked about the money, Kate could give no explanation. There were old newspapers, unopened letters, and junk mail, all strewn throughout the downstairs rooms. At the rear of the house the briars had become so invasive that the back door could not be opened. The interior of the house in general was filthy and the toilet was broken. Why hadn't Theresa informed her siblings?

Since Oliver death, Theresa and Adrian had brought Kate to their own home for the weekends. Annie learned later that Theresa would ring Kate every Friday evening to tell her that Adrian was on his way to pick her up. Kate would put on her coat and be waiting at the gate when his car arrived. After spending the weekend with Theresa and Adrian, Kate would be dropped back at her own gate on the Sunday evening. Rarely had anyone looked inside Kate's house to see how she was living. *She was flying under the radar*

Once a month, Kate would go by train to Limerick, to spend a weekend with Anthony, and the next month she would go to Cork for a weekend with Thomas. This arrangement had worked until she started to get on the wrong train, sending all concerned into such a panic. Annie was shocked at how her mother's health had declined. She was angry with herself for being on the other side of the world, but most of all, she was at a loss as to how things could have so *quietly* deteriorated.

She called in on Kate's neighbour's who, though surprised, were also pleased to learn that Kate had family. They confirmed to Annie that a man, in a car, picked Kate up every Friday and dropped her back on Sunday. They added that they had never seen him get out of the car. Annie canvassed other neighbours and most of them thought that the house had become derelict and was unoccupied.

Annie asked the parish priest to keep an eye on Kate, and maybe make his parishioners aware of the degree of her sickness. Later she spoke with the staff in the post office, the supermarket, and the grocers, and while doing so, gave them the phone numbers of Theresa and Anthony, in case they ever found Kate in trouble. Having done this, Annie arranged for the community nurse to call on Kate.

Annie had noticed Kate was rubbing her tummy a lot, and that her knees were troubling her. When Kate refused to go to the doctors, Annie rang the surgery and explained that if the doctor herself were to ring and invite Kate to come in for a routine blood test, she might agree. It worked and Annie and Kate left the surgery armed with four referrals for four different specialists.

While visiting Anthony's family in Limerick, Anthony's wife

Pam, volunteered to help Annie clean Kate's house. It was a big offer that would involve a three-hour bus journey. When Annie and Pam arrived at the house, armed with cleaning gear, they were surprised to find Theresa there. During the eight years their mother had lived alone, Theresa had not once helped her clean the house. So why now?

Kate began to stress with all the attention so Annie hugged her, "Sure, we're only doing a bit of tidying up mum."

They discovered the untouched coal in the outside bunker. It was purchased by Oliver just before he died. Pam and Annie worked for hours scrubbing and cleaning, while Theresa went through the motions with a duster. A skip arrived outside and the huge task of clearing out eight years of household rubbish began. While Theresa and Pam tackled Kate's bedroom Annie took her mother to the local shop to buy some ham and cheese for lunch. On their return, Pam announced that the bed sheets were putrid and were only fit for the skip. She told Annie that they had found yet more money squirreled away in the bed. The total reached almost five thousand, Euro's in the new currency. Theresa took some of this money, called a taxi, and went shopping for new bedding, a small fridge, a kettle, and a few smaller items. Annie asked her to bank the remainder of their mother's money.

Later that day while scrubbing the bath, Annie heard Theresa complaining that, her back was broke. Looking over her shoulder she watched her climbing the stairs on all fours. 'What a fucking drama queen,' thought Annie. 'We did all the hard work and there she is on all fours. Jesus, she makes me so mad.

Theresa called it quits for the day and suggested that Annie and Pam go back to her place for dinner. "What about mam?" Annie asked.

"She'll be alright. She'll see us when we come back in the morning."

"We can't leave her in this mess," Annie protested. Theresa reluctantly agreed, and the four women went by taxi to Theresa's home.

Soon after they arrived, Adrian asked Kate, if she had a nice lunch?"

"Yes," she answered.

"What did you have?" he pressed. Her face showed quite clearly that she couldn't remember.

"Um-um-um… I had a pie," she stammered.

"You had a pie, did you?" he smirked. "And what kind of pie did you have?"

"Um, it was a curry pie." Annie felt anger toward him.

"Leave her alone," she snapped. With this he turned to Theresa with a grin that said, 'we got the two birds there, with just the one stone.'

Earlier that year Anthony had noticed deterioration in Kate's health and suggested to Thomas that she was in need of help.

Kate was in hospital at one stage, with high blood pressure and the two brothers travelled to Dublin to see her. After their visit they went to Ballyfermot to take a look at the family home. They were shocked and horrified at what they found. Mice droppings everywhere, the house was filthy and cluttered. Thomas went upstairs to use the loo and ran back down, gagging. Excrement floated in an un-flushable toilet bowl. On the verge of vomiting, he rang Adrian to come over and fix it.

Thomas and Anthony lived several hours drive from Kate. Anthony had been on the telephone and discussed with Theresa, Kate's need for assistance, suggesting at least a few hours every week. Theresa's response was a disinterested, "yep-yep." Anthony also rang Annie in Australia, explaining what he had observed at Kate's home. Annie remembered the promise she made several years earlier, and she felt that the time was nigh.

Chapter Six

It was the last weekend in June 2009. Annie and two girl friends were having a holiday break at her property in country NSW. The girls were laughing and storytelling in front of the fire when Annie received a text from Theresa in Ireland. It read, *"Are you at home?"* The ambiguity of the message had only concerned Annie a little, and coupled with bad reception, and an amount of alcohol having been drunk, it would be the following day when she called Theresa. It was during that call; she discovered that Kate had collapsed. Kate suffered arthritis in both knees and had been at the local health centre to pick up a walker relater. Theresa had decided to walk Kate, using her new contraption. It was an unusually hot day and, while wearing an over coat, Kate became overwhelmed with the heat and collapsed, requiring an ambulance to take her to the hospital.

Some time later, Annie and Greg were helping their neighbour move house. The neighbour told them how he had managed to find a high paying tenant to rent his house. Annie took down the name of the real estate agent, and an appointment was made.

When the agent told Annie and Greg how much rent their well situated house would return, they were pleasantly surprised. Greg's mother in Sydney had moved into a nursing home, leaving her own house empty, and for the time being, Greg would be able to live there rent free. This was a major break for Annie. Excited, she rang Theresa in Ireland. "Guess what? She said, "I'm coming home, on a one way ticket!" The silence that followed, was audible

"Are you still there," Annie asked.

"Why are you coming back?" asked Theresa.

"To help mam."

"But you know she stays with us!"

"Yes Theresa. I'm aware that she stays with you for two days a week. That leaves five days, where she is on her own."

"But she's grand!"

"Well," said Annie, "from what Anthony tells me, she is anything but grand. She's my mother too," Annie continued, "and I promised her that I'd come home and help her when she needed me."

"Why now?" persisted Theresa.

"Because things are falling apart for her, and besides, it's what I do for a living, I want to spend some quality time caring for her, before she forgets who I am. Theresa, I love my mother and I'm going to honour a vow I made to her a long time ago."

As soon as Theresa hung up from Annie, she rang Adrian. "Guess what? Annie's coming home, to live in Ballyfermot."

"You are joking?"

"What the fuck are we going to do Adrian?"

"Don't worry, leave it with me," he said. 'Give me time to think."

Theresa spent the larger part of that afternoon pacing, and winding her self into a tsunami. When Adrian arrived home her nerves were in pieces. "What are we going to do? Who the fuck does she think she is, swanning back here after all these years?"

"Settle down," he reasoned. "We have plenty of time. I've been thinking: Firstly, you go to the bank and change the address on your mum's statements. Have them posted here. Get your mother to sign you up as her collecting agent for the pension. Then as soon as she's discharged from hospital, we'll bring her to live here. Nobody would have a clue. She's already here two days a week. How could anyone prove she's not here full time? I'll check with Social Welfare about the carer pension. Whatever their cut off is, we'll make sure your sister has no chance of getting it."

"Fuck her," said Theresa.

"Now!" said Adrian, while increasing in confidence. "The final nail in your sister's coffin will be for you to get your mother to appoint you, as her Enduring Power of Attorney. That way we'll have complete power over her estate. I'll make an appointment with the solicitor in the morning. Fuck all of them! It's you and me babe! We're the only ones that do anything for her. They all fucked off and didn't care about the rest of us." Adrian hugged Theresa, "It'll be fine, sugar plum, you'll see."

Theresa later rang Thomas to tell him of Annie's impending visit. She told him that Kate would be staying with herself and Adrian, for at least three days every week, and that nothing would change that fact. She remarked to Thomas, that Annie was coming home because *she wanted to be remembered.*

The following day, after hearing the news, Anthony phoned Theresa and suggested, that on Annie's return, all four siblings should get together to discuss their mother's welfare. "That's fine," she replied, "but I'll be having mam three days a week, and that's final."

"That should be a family decision," he said.

"That may well be, but I'm having mam three days every week, and that's the way it will be."

"Theresa, let's just wait until Annie gets here so we can all discuss what's best for mam". Theresa screamed down the phone,

"Fuck off…" and then hung up.

Chapter Seven

It was the first week in July in Australia and the tenants applying to rent Annie's house, had requested a contract for a minimum of three years. This arrangement would leave Annie and Greg with no mortgage worries for the near future. At last Annie felt that she could honour the promise to her mother. It would be Greg's 50th birthday in the September, and plans were already afoot to throw him a big party. Annie's temporary move to Ireland meant she would need to make arrangements with her two employers for leave without pay. Anthony had spoken to the Irish Social Welfare about Annie coming home to take care of their mother. He explained that she was a trained Dementia Specific Nurse with many years experience, adding, how she and her mother had worked together as volunteers in care groups for Dementia sufferers. The girl from the 'department of social welfare' told Anthony, that because Annie was away from Ireland for so long, she didn't qualify for carer's pension, however, they would consider an application under what they called 'extenuating circumstances' and would send him out the relevant paperwork.

Anthony had arranged for Annie to purchase a cheap trade in car from a contact he had in Limerick. She scraped enough frequent flyer points together to pay for a one-way flight to Ireland. It was agreed that Greg would join her during the following March to celebrate her fiftieth birthday.

Annie was so looking forward to spending time with Kate. She felt she had a lot of making up to do. Always the romantic dreamer she planned to drive her mother all over Ireland, while spoiling her at every opportunity. She had a strong romantic notion that her re-united family were going to have the best Christmas ever.

Because the arranged car was in Limerick, she flew into Shannon. Anthony and his two children (Grace and Sean) met her at the airport. Anthony's wife Pam had prepared a baked dinner and Annie was on a great high as she told everyone, how wonderful it was to be back home. She spoke with Anthony on all matters, including Theresa. She told him of Theresa's reaction, of silence, to her homecoming news. "Theresa's, '*oh shit!*' moment," he remarked. Annie had not heard from her other brother, Thomas. She had expected maybe a phone call. She rang Theresa in Dublin and received a curt response. During that phone call, she got to chat with her mum and told her that she would be there soon to see her.

The following day Annie took the initiative and phoned Thomas. When she told him she would be taking Kate on a road trip, she felt his reaction was strangely cool.

While waiting for her car to be prepared, (a few minor problems) she helped Anthony with his house painting. Theresa rang her there and accused her of not caring for their mother. Her logic being that Annie had flown into Shannon instead of Dublin. Annie tried to explain that it was more practical to go where the car was to be picked up. Annie was trying to explain to Theresa how unreasonable her accusations were sounding, when Theresa hung up.

The car was finally ready and Annie waved good-bye to Anthony and his family in Limerick. She had told them that she would return with Kate for a holiday. On the drive to Dublin she stopped for a picnic and felt herself reconnecting with the flora and fauna of her native country. Closing her eyes she took in deep breaths of the sweet smelling peat filled air. She was back: This was her *beautiful Ireland*, ancient mountains, landscapes filled to brimming with amazing stories, the rich smell of the grasses and the magical soul soothing sounds of its unique nature. She felt at peace.

On reaching Dodder Valley, in Dublin, she found Adrian's car parked in the driveway. Theresa answered her knock, and again her greeting was curt. No hug. No smile. It was as if she was contemptuous of her. When Kate saw Annie, they hugged and hugged. Adrian sat on the sofa and said little. Annie tried in vain to make polite chit chat before finally inviting Kate to come with her. Kate then said, as if rehearsed, "I don't live in Ballyfermot; I live in Dodder Valley Estate. I stay here, in Dodder Valley."

"That's ok mam," said Annie, trying to reassure her. "It's Anthony's birthday during the week, and he said, he would love to see you. Kate immediately stood up.

"Oh that would be nice Annie." Adrian jumped up and flayed his arms, saying,

"You are not taking your mother from this house. She lives with us now. She will not be going with you and that's final" Annie was horrified. Kate then pointed at Annie; her expression was one of stress, as she looked from Adrian to Annie

"I want to go with you. I want to be where you live."

"Kate goes to Day-care now," interjected Adrian. "Why should she break her routine just for you?"

"Because I'm her daughter, because she wants to come with me." Annie turned to Kate, and continued, "Mam, you go to your day-care tomorrow. Theresa will inform the staff that your daughter Annie will be taking you on a small holiday." Theresa reacted angrily.

"She is going to take you to Ballyfermot, she is lying Mam, she wants to take you back there." Annie held Kate's hand.

"Mam, I will pick you up tomorrow, after day care, and I promise you, we will go to Anthony's for his birthday." Kate hugged her.

Driving away without Kate was painful for Annie and she was at a loss to understand why Adrian and Theresa had been so cold and defensive. Annie felt she didn't know the rules of whatever the family game was meant to be. She felt she had no choice but to walk away. Why wouldn't Kate want to live in Ballyfermot? Ballyfermot was her home. Many questions presented as Annie drove towards her old home.

Arriving outside the house on Spiddal Road, she immediately felt its emptiness; it stood dishevelled and unwelcoming, and did indeed look derelict. The driveway was blocked by an overgrown shrub and was inaccessible by car. When she opened the door of the porch, she stepped on weeks of un-opened mail. As she opened the main door and stepped into the hallway, she felt the, full gut wrenching, silent scream of neglect. The house they had worked so hard to make liveable the previous year, had yet again been allowed to sink into neglect. There was no power. The fridge stank and it was cultivating mould. 'So, this is my welcome home,' she sighed, as her eyes welled with tears. She felt uncertain if the electricity company had disconnected the power or if it was just turned off in the metre. She knocked on the neighbouring door. "Hi, I'm not sure if you remember me, I'm Annie, Kate's daughter from Australia. The young neighbour introduced himself as Marty and invited Annie inside to meet his wife, Tina. Annie told the couple of her plans, and of her problem with the power. Marty immediately offered to check the power and left Annie and Tina to reacquaint over a cup of tea. "How is your mum? We've been so worried about her," asked Tina.

She's okay. I just saw her this afternoon, and she's as well as can be expected." Marty returned.

"It was switched off at the mains," he said. "It's grand now."

"Thank you so much," said Annie, "I really do appreciate your help." Tina insisted that Annie stay for another cup of tea and the three discussed all manner of topics, including Kate.

"We haven't seen Kate since the end of June," said Marty.

"Yes," replied Annie, while doing a mental calculation. "That would have been when she collapsed over on Blackditch road. From the hospital my sister took her to live at their house. It seems, they have had a change of heart and now they don't want her to live back here."

"Why?" asked Tina. "She's lived here for years."

"More than fifty two years," said Annie. "I told my sister when mam was hospitalised that I would look after her in her own home. However, she has her plans, and I'm not privy to them."

"It doesn't make sense," continued Tina. "This is your mother's world. It's where she belongs." Marty informed Annie that the previous year he was having trouble with a rank smell which appeared to emanate from his back bedroom. He was ready to pull up the floor boards, when a friend suggested it was coming from Kate's house. It turned out to be Kate's toilet that was the cause.

"I shudder when I think how my mum was subject to such neglect," said Annie. "And I'm at a loss as to why Theresa and her husband are so hostile to me. I'm hoping, now that I am home, the situation will settle down."

Annie felt tired after the day she had gone through. The bedroom in her mother's house was cold but her tiredness overtook her and she drifted off to sleep.

As Kate was attending day care until 3:00 pm, Annie decided after breakfast the following morning, that she would tackle the monster shrub in the driveway. Mr Dunne, Annie's elderly next door neighbour, welcomed her home and provided her with all manner of garden implements. Tina on the other side brought her a piping hot coffee and a piece of cake. Several more neighbours stopped along their journey and chatted with Annie, all of them enquiring after her mother's health. The neighbourhood friendliness buoyed Annie's spirit and she managed a productive morning's work.

Lunch and a chat with Mrs Dunne brought a welcomed rest for Annie. They laughed and talked on past events in the neighbourhood, including Oliver's passing and of Kate's declining health. Mrs Dunne on a couple of occasions spoke of Annie's nature, "You are so like your mum," she told her, "your natures are identical. Not that I have anything against your siblings, but Annie, you are the definitely the 'chip off the old block', if you know what I mean?"

Annie thanked the Dunne's for their kindness and promised to bring Kate by, for a visit. Mrs Dunne hugged her, and repeated how pleased she was that she had come home. "It really is the best thing you could do for your mum; she will be comforted by your presence."

As Annie listened to soft music on her drive towards Dodder valley, suspicion returned, concerning Theresa's anger the previous day. There had to be a reason why she was behaving so defensively over Kate? While Annie waited for Kate's return from day-care, Theresa launched yet another personal attack on her.

***

One year earlier while on holidays in Ireland, Annie had spent the first week with Theresa and Kate in Dodder valley. The second week she had planned to be with Anthony and his family in Limerick. Anthony had arranged time off work for the occasion. Theresa decided that she would like to go along for the trip. Anthony felt strongly that she should not join them, and should instead, allow Annie to spend this quality time with him and his family. 'This would be practical,' he had suggested, as there would not be enough room, in the car, to transport an extra person around the countryside. While speaking to Annie on the phone, he asked if she would ask Theresa not come. Annie replied that she would broach the delicate subject when she felt the timing was right. Later that evening Anthony rang again and asked if she had spoken to Theresa, "Not yet," she replied, "but I will."

As soon as the call ended, she approached Theresa. "That was Anthony. He was wondering if, on this occasion, you didn't come to Limerick, as he wishes to spend some quality time with me." Anthony's rejection was more than Theresa could take and her countenance turned livid.

"How come he never wants quality time with me?" she roared, as her face reddened.

"Perhaps it's because he see's you throughout the year and he doesn't get to see me that often." Annie tried to minimise Theresa's hurt by suggesting that she follow on Friday, with Kate on the train. At this suggestion Theresa turned to face Annie.

"I'm not going anywhere with mam. It's a break from her that I want!"

After arriving in Limerick Annie rang Theresa again suggesting that it would be nice if she could make it down with Kate. Annie added that Thomas was coming from Cork and that way Kate would have all her children together. "I can't come! I'm busy!" she replied.

***

One year on and Theresa brought up the subject of how Annie never wanted her to go to Limerick. "Actually," replied Annie, "It was Anthony who wanted time out with me. I was just the messenger." Theresa screamed back at her.

"You're a fucking liar! It was you!" Annie shook her head in frustration. Theresa went on to accuse her of heading off to Australia and not caring what happened to their mother.

"That is so unfair," said Annie. "I have always cared about mam, and moving to another country doesn't make me any less caring. That's why I'm back! To care for her as I promised I would." Theresa muttered,

"I'm sure you really care." This remark incensed Annie.

"Had I stayed in Dublin," she said, "I would not have allowed our mother to live alone, like a sewer rat, on Spiddal Road." At this point Adrian entered the argument.

"It is unfair of you to suggest neglect by Theresa. There are two other siblings living in Ireland. Why don't they clean your mum's house?" Annie looked at him.

"All I can say to that is, if I lived this close to mam, I would have helped her. Her house is an absolute disgrace." Annie took a breath. "Why can't we stop squabbling?" she said, "and do what's best for her?"

At this offering of the 'olive branch,' Theresa mellowed and offered to make Annie a cup of tea. Annie still felt an underlying tension but decided to try and play the game. Kate was due shortly and she didn't want her to be privy to their squabbling.

Adrian began a new conversation. "You could have bowled me over with a feather," he said, "when your mother asked, why don't you put a tenant in my house?" Annie feigned surprise.

"Wow! Did mam really ask you that? Well I never!" she answered, as more alarm bells began sounding. In a thousand years, Annie would not have believed that Kate could say such a thing: Firstly, there was her lifelong attachment to her home, and secondly, her mind could not have grasped the concept of 'tenants and renting.' Annie believed that Adrian was planting the seed of his intent.

While a carer helped Kate from the bus, Annie introduced herself. She informed the carer that Kate would be spending a week in Limerick, and asked that the message be passed on to her office.

Back inside the house, Annie had asked for Kate's tablets, and had begun writing the medication details down, when she heard Theresa call her name. When she turned, Theresa threw her arms around her. "I love you Annie," she said, "I am so glad you are home. I really am." Tears actually appeared in Theresa's eyes. Annie stood dumbfounded. Theresa then took hold of Annie's silver necklace, "Is this 'real Tiffany?" she asked. Annie looked through her crocodile tears.

"Nah," she answered, "It's fake, definitely fake."

Chapter Eight

At last Annie was alone with Kate. She drove until she was out of sight of Theresa's house and stopped. "Mum," she began with childlike excitement, "we are going to have so much fun. We are going to take trips all over the country. We'll share Christmas in both Cork and Limerick with the boys. This car is for you mam. This car will take you wherever your heart desires. If the Pope can have his 'Popemobile' then Kate will have her very own 'Katemobile.' Kate became overwhelmed with happiness and excitement and she reached out and took Annie's hand.

While leaving the city behind, Kate expressed her love for the trees and countryside. She pointed to cloud formations, while remarking, "I can see shapes up there." Mother and daughter sang, talked, and laughed while stopping occasionally for coffee and pee-breaks. "Look up Annie, there's a ship." Annie looked, and to her astonishment, there was indeed a pirate ship in the clouds. This moment, though small, filled Annie with great joy.

Kate cried with happiness, as she hugged Anthony and his family, and later that evening they all sat down to a traditional Irish dinner, in a room that sang with laughter, during recollections of amusing family memories.

Kate's grandchildren, Grace and Sean were most kind to their grandmother. Anthony had already explained to them that she was unwell, and that certain things might aggravate her. The children quickly learned that she couldn't cope with open doors. She would jump up and close them when the children forgot. If the children were boisterous, she would become agitated. Despite this, the children competed to bring her coffee and to sit beside her at the dinner table.

Kate loved it when Anthony took her to mass on the Sunday morning. Later that afternoon, the family went for a drive in the country. Grace and Sean loved travelling in the Katemobile, and joined in when Annie started an Irish sing-a-long. Annie marvelled at the joy on Kate's face. It was at this time that she fully realised that Kate now lived, in 'the moment'. She could be happy in the moment. That evening Kate's memory of their day in the country was lost to her.

Sometime later, Annie rang Thomas to let him know that they were in Limerick. She told him that she and Kate would be heading to Cork to catch up with him. She felt that he was a little frosty; nevertheless, they set a day and time.

Arriving in Cork they met Thomas on the roadside. He hugged both of them and they followed his car to his home.

The family gathered, and over dinner they all made general conversation. In a quiet moment alone with Thomas, Annie tried to broach the subject of Theresa's behaviour, but he quickly brushed her off. Again there was that underlying tension.

The next morning Thomas made breakfast and was quick to tell them that they should leave before the traffic got bad. Annie got the message. They said their goodbyes and she and Kate left for Dublin.

Annie took her time along this journey, in a bid to enjoy the last few hours with Kate.

Theresa had quiet strongly stated that Kate would be staying with herself and Adrian for three days every week; Sunday afternoon until Wednesday afternoon. Annie could pick her up Wednesday at 3:00 pm, and Theresa and Adrian would collect her on the following Sunday at 3:00 pm. This arrangement was none negotiable.

As they neared Dublin, Annie decided to take Kate to Spiddal Road in Ballyfermot. She was interested to see her reaction. On their arrival Kate beamed a smile and declared, "This is my house."

"It sure is," replied Annie, as she took Kate's hand and led her inside. The week prior, Annie had spent some time tiding the house and when Kate walked into the lounge room, her eyes filled with tears.

"This is my home. These are my things," she said, sitting and smiling at the room. Annie had questions: 'What had been said to Kate about this house?' Why was she frightened of Ballyfermot? Had they used her years of loneliness as a way of scaring her?' After sharing a meal at the kitchen table, Annie told Kate that she had to take her back to Theresa's. "Why can't I live here with you?" she asked. Annie had no answer for her.

Chapter Nine

On their arrival at Dodder valley, Theresa greeted Kate with a smile. "Welcome back to '*your home*' mam," she said, trying to make a point.

"No," snapped Annie. "Ballyfermot is her home." Adrian joined in, stating that Kate now lived with them and had done so for the last two years. "Really," continued Annie, "I was home last year and mam lived in Ballyfermot."

"Then, she has lived with us for a year."

"That's not true either," Annie corrected. "When I call her on the phone, from Australia, she answers in Ballyfermot."

"Well, she's lived with us for six months then."

"Her neighbours in Spiddal road told me she was at home when they went on a holiday in June and when they returned she was gone." There was complete silence as Annie, her face now livid, showed complete contempt for the insult thrown at her intelligence. "So, what's it going to be," she continued, "two years, one year, or maybe six months? Adrian and Theresa were dumbfounded. "I put it to you," concluded Annie, "My mother has only lived in this house since the day I informed you that I was coming home. An amazing coincidence, don't you think?" Annie turned her back on Theresa and Adrian, walked into the adjoining room, hugged Kate goodnight, and left the house.

While driving back to Ballyfermot, her suspicions began to focus on matters of finance. Presumably Kate had an aged pension? Where was it going? Her electricity account showed credits, she has free travel and no rent to pay. Annie also noted that Kate's mail didn't include bank statements or any other correspondence from the bank. She decided to find out exactly what was happening with Kate's money. It had been over a year since they found the five thousand Euros.' Could she have squirreled more away since that time? Annie resolved to take Kate to the bank and clear things up.

The taking back of Kate to Theresa's, had become a major downer for Annie. She decided to kill her time alone, by giving the house a makeover. She began stripping wallpaper and continued into the early hours. Taking on the house had proved to be a formidable task: The lace curtains were filthy and torn; the kitchen linoleum was beyond redemption and, what seemed like a thousand other jobs were lined up waiting. She had asked Theresa to buy a piece of linoleum for the kitchen; a hundred Euros would have covered it. It never got done. The toilet remained broken and Annie had to roll up her sleeve and press down the ball cock in order to flush the cistern. Conditions were not in keeping with modern Ireland. 'How could it have come to this,' she asked herself: Ireland has gone through The Celtic Tiger, money was plentiful, the population enjoyed comforts like they had never seen before, the government renovated the old council houses, fitting them out with down stairs toilets and bedrooms; mainly to aid the aged, and yet, here was Kate, the woman who would share a crumb with a bird, being subjected to live in third world conditions. Hadn't anybody noticed the wheels falling off of her world? Why didn't a hand go up for Kate? She suffered Arthritis in both knees, making the stairs difficult, and on top of that, the winters were freezing. Annie cried at the lack of care, including her own ignorance at what was a complete travesty of the word CARE. She remembered the look on Kate's face when Adrian refused to let her leave the house and it made her rip at the wall-paper.

On day two she began painting. Her neighbour Marty was a taxi driver. Annie was on a ladder painting when the headlights pulled into his driveway at 3:00 am. It was at this point she realised that she had been avoiding the lonely nights by working. The nights were the worst: Manic work, fatigue, and then sleep. She looked at a piece of miss-matched carpet and it reminded her of Oliver. Lifting it revealed a footprint on the floorboards of the dividing wall that had once separated her siblings. She became annoyed that she had to kill her time like this, when all she longed for was to be with Kate.

During the daylight hours she would walk up and down the town. Her three days of separation felt like months. When she arrived to pick up Kate, Theresa's friend Betty was there. The tension became palpable. Had Theresa brought this woman to her house, for moral support? Kate remained seated, with her handbag in her lap. Theresa offered a cup of tea and Betty tried to engage Annie in chit-chat. Annie felt a contradiction between their civility and the atmosphere. She asked Kate if she was ready to go home, Theresa snapped, "She is home. She is only going to visit you." Annie felt disappointed with Theresa, and for Kate sake, she held her tongue.

On leaving, she informed Theresa that the chimney at Spiddal Road needed cleaning. Theresa replied that Kate had money in her purse, and she could pay for it.

Arriving back on Spiddal Road, Annie took Kate to see Mrs. Dunne. When the two women, who had been neighbours for over fifty-two years, were reunited, they put their walking sticks aside, hugged each other in the warmest embrace, and wept openly. A couple of hours passed as they drank tea and reminisced of times and people from their past.

Later Annie stood behind Kate and watched as she struggled, step by step, to climb her own stairs. A question struck Annie: 'Had she remained in Australia, would Theresa still have taken Kate anyway from Spiddal Road?' Had she not, Kate would have been struggling alone in much the same manner. Annie knew she would never get an answer to this question and it bothered her.

One year earlier, Anthony had telephoned the Alzheimer's Association to explain Kate's condition and to enquire as to what course of action should be taken. They told him that Kate ideally should remain in her own home as long as possible, adding that the familiarity of home, along with community and friends, would prove much better for her.

The next morning Annie awoke to find Kate staring straight at her. "You are here! Oh thank God. I had a dream that you were here. It's so wonderful."

"I'm here mum. It's not a dream. I am here; I'm with you."

Mrs Dunne, had told Annie to call in at the Citizens Advice Bureau, as they could offer advice on her mother's entitlements.

There was a look of delight on Kate's face, when Annie said, "The Katemobile is at your disposal mam." Annie fastened her seat-belt. "Wherever you want to go, just say the word, and I will take you there." Kate then gave a set of red beads and a crucifix to Annie.

"They will keep us safe," she said. Annie smiled and hung them from the rear view mirror.

Kate was driven to her local church where she quickly became surrounded by friends and acquaintances, all expressing their concern for her. Several people remarked that they had not seen her for a couple of months. Annie was overwhelmed with the kindness shown to Kate. "You're a super star, just like Angelina Jolie," she whispered. Kate then led the way to a particular pew in the chapel, where a brass plaque, in remembrance of Oliver Murray, had been placed. The inscription read '*Please, pray for his soul.*' Annie had commissioned the plaque when she was home for her father's funeral. This was the place where Kate always sat.

The young priest spotted Kate from the altar and acknowledged her with a smile. Annie had spoken to the priest on her previous visit.

When mass was over, he approached Kate and asked how she had been. "I've been good Father," she answered. "This is my daughter Annie."

"We spoke last year,' said Annie. " I sat in your car out of the rain.

"You live in Australia."

"I do father. I've come home to be with mum for a while."

"I'm sure Kate is delighted to have you with her. She's a great woman your mother and I can assure you that she is much loved, by all in this church.

After Kate and Annie left the church they drove to the bank where Annie began to explain Kate's situation. She told the teller that she suspected something was not quite right with her mum's financial affairs. The teller asked if she wanted past statements and suggested maybe two years.

"That would be great," said Annie, and went on to ask why Kate was not receiving statements at Spiddal Road.

"The address was changed to Tallaght, Dodder Valley." the teller said, while looking at her computer.

"Really? And when was that?"

"Early July." The teller then turned to Kate. "Would you like a bank card?" Kate smiled.

"Thank you," she said, "that would be nice." The teller asked Annie if she would like her name on the card.

"God no! My mum needs to be left with some independence, however, I will be coming in with her to withdraw money to fix up the house, and I intend keeping every receipt."

"Good idea," agreed the teller.

The next stop was the citizen's advice bureau, where an assistant introduced herself as Margaret O'Callaghan, before going on to explain that she was not a Care Officer but a part of the advocate team, adding that she had only stepped in because they were busy. This twist of fate proved to be a blessing, because by the end of the discussion Margaret O'Callaghan had become Kate's personal advocate. She gave Annie leaflets on several different organisations that might prove useful to Kate. Annie felt that things were starting to happen.

In the same building, Kate and Annie found a café, where they indulged in tea and scones. Kate never tired of telling Annie how happy she was to have her home.

That night Annie lay in bed thinking about Theresa, and what she might be up to with Kate's finances. She hated the fact that she was having these thoughts. She hated the fact that Kate had become an innocent victim, not only of Theresa and Adrian and the cruel hand of nature, but worse, a victim of a family fight, that she herself felt necessary to make things right. But things won't ever be right, she told herself, before drifting off to sleep.

Morning came and the previous night's melancholia had left. Kate and Annie were enjoying boiled eggs and toast, and smiling, like life really was wonderful. "What would you like to do today?" Annie asked.

"I usually go to mass," she replied. Annie looked at her and stood up from the table.

"Let's go then. We can't be late for Father John." They both laughed.

When they arrived in the church yard, Kate hugged and cried as she met her friends, as if for the first time.

Again during the mass, Kate stepped out into the aisle to hug those same people as they were returning from communion. It made Annie sad to see the shock and confusion on their faces.

After mass Kate and Annie headed down to the main street, where they enjoyed an alfresco coffee, while a man played accordion music. As they lingered and listened, even more people stopped to greet Kate.

"Mam," said Annie. "The accordion man is playing Parisian music. If we use our imagination, we could be in 'Gay Paris.'" They both laughed at the thought.

Later in the afternoon, Annie watched Kate searching the house for something. "Dear God, I can't find it," she said. "I don't know where my pension book is. " What will I do? Dear God help me?"

Annie telephoned Theresa and said. "Mam can't find her pension book."

"She appointed me her collecting agent," replied Theresa. "It's not a book anymore. Tell her, I collect her pension, and she doesn't have a book anymore." Annie told Kate what Theresa had said.

"Well she's very smart, isn't she?" replied Kate.

Later that evening, Annie watched as Kate searched once more for her pension book. Searching her handbag, going through cupboards and drawers, looking behind photos. Annie became upset, while watching her mum's futile search.

She rang Anthony and explained the situation. "Ring Theresa back," he said. "Let her know the stress she is causing mam. Tell her to explain it to mam, herself." Annie did as he suggested.

The next day they went to the local shops. The grocery shop doubles as a sub post office. This is where Kate had collected her pension for years. While Kate was busy speaking to the grocer, Annie spoke to the Postmaster, explaining that Kate did not have a book or a card. He searched his computer. "Your mam signed a form appointing Theresa McGee to be her collecting agent."

"When?" asked Annie.

"Early July."

"So," said Annie, "a simple signature, on a form that Kate couldn't possibly understand, and her pension is given away."

Annie rang the department of Social Welfare and was told that Kate signed the form. They went on to tell Annie to write a letter asking for her mother's pension to be reinstated, and to get Kate to sign it. Annie huffed as she said, "She has Alzheimer's. And you're suggesting that I get her to sign a letter that was constructed by me. I rest my case.

As Annie sat alone in front of the fire, childhood memories resurfaced. The house had seemed bigger back then. Looking around, she wondered how the six of them had shared such a tiny fireplace. Once upon a time the house sparkled. She went up the staircase removing photos of herself and her siblings from the walls. She opened drawers and cupboards and gathered more pictures. It took her several hours but she covered an entire downstairs wall with family photographs. She called it, 'Kate's wall of memories.'

She sent a text message to her cousin Liam, letting him know she was home. He arrived within the hour. Liam was a favourite; she loved his sense of humour. She related to him what was happening with Theresa and Adrian. "I remember as a child," he commented, "coming to visit Aunty Kate, and being afraid to drop a crumb. I am shocked at the neglect."

"It was a lot worse than this," said Annie. "I've cleaned the heavy stuff."

She showed him the toilet and what she has to do to flush it. "You're joking!" he said. "I'll bring my neighbour tomorrow. He works for the Corporation, refurbishing the older houses. He may have a new toilet, or maybe he can fix this one. Liam began to reminisce about the old days and he had Annie laughing with joy. She was riding a roller-coaster of emotions and the higher she climbed the further she was going to fall.

After he left, her mood took a dive. In her mind, she could hear the key turning in the lock. She imagined her father swaying and staring at each family member in turn.

While looking at the photo's, on the wall, it struck her how different everyone was. Anthony was the intelligent sibling, the one that did well at school. Theresa was brighter than her, and had a definite need to dominate. Thomas always looked sad.

Oliver and Kate had adopted Thomas as a baby. Annie adored him. Oliver would be heard to say, tactlessly to casual visitors, 'This is Thomas, my adopted son.' Kate was always neat and smart, and Oliver always wore a tailored shirt and tie. Annie smiled as an image entered her head of Oliver walking on Bondi Beach, while wearing his suit and shiny shoes. Old photos of grandparents, great grandparents, aunts, uncles and cousins, were included in the gallery that was now the wall of Kate's life.

Annie felt weary as she climbed the stairs, and cold as she put her hand in the cistern to flush the loo. In bed she fought images of her ghosts and she began to cry into her pillow. When she was a child, her mother would come into her room to seek refuge from Oliver. She would sit quietly on the edge of the bed, and Annie would listen as Oliver, from the other side of the door, made his demands on Kate. She would beg her mother to stay, but Kate always gave in to Oliver. 'Those were such confusing times' she told herself as she drifted off to sleep.

The following morning came cool and crisp for Annie, and as she talked and hummed to herself, her voice echoed around the sparsely furnished room. While stoking the fire, she made the decision that she would clean the entire house.

Where to start? Opening up a side cupboard, she picked out a small red biscuit tin. On the kitchen table lay a receipt from the chimney sweep. She placed it inside the tin. Keep every receipt, she reminded herself.

For several hours she lost herself in the endless cleaning. Feeling like a break, she remembered Mrs Dunne telling her, if she needed company, to call anytime. She also felt sad that she hadn't got to be her mother's full time carer; she was now the one her mother visited for half a week. She was feeling uneasy in her own company and decided she would pay the Dunne's a visit.

Again Mrs. Dunne remembered Annie as a child, and talked of how mischievous she was, and once again stating that she had her mother's nature. This sweet line buoyed Annie's spirit. Mrs. Dunne's daughter arrived. Apparently, she came every Wednesdays and Friday, one day to do housework and the other to do grocery shopping. She told Annie that in all the years since Oliver died, she had not seen Theresa pay Kate one visit. From the Dunne's kitchen window, Kate's back yard embarrassed Annie, and again she promised that she would address the problem just as soon as she found help. She thanked them for their company and left.

Kate had accumulated lots of clothing that she could never wear again. During the previous year, the task of bagging them had been started by herself, Pam and Theresa. All three women agreed Kate would never, and could never, wear all these clothes. What was bagged was given to the Charity Shop. What didn't get bagged, was not touched again. It was now one year on and there was still plenty of work left to do in the house. This work, for Annie proved a welcomed distraction.

Later in the afternoon Liam arrived with a friend. Annie gave them the grizzly tour of the toilet and the back yard "Jesus! How on earth did she ever use the clothes line?"

"I'm guessing she didn't." said Annie. "Look at my legs, will you? They're scratched to bits from hanging the clothes out. If mum, had fallen into the briars, she could have been found dead"

"Bastards," said Liam. "They should have been charged."
After the boys left, Annie felt the enormity of it all. The garden was beyond her. The weeds alone were as high as trees. She made a list of the calls she would make the following day.

Her evenings alone in the house hit hard. She had been known as the peace maker of the family. She wasn't equipped for whatever Theresa was contriving. The friendliness from the fireplace and her family pictures looking down from the gallery, were her only solace.

Next morning, while walking down the main street of Ballyfermot, memories rekindled for Annie. She was getting out of the house more and more, in a bid to fill the long lonely days. In the town she saw tired and weathered faces that belonged in her childhood. She sat at the 'Parisian' café and waited for the man to serenade her, but he didn't come. She walked the long way back to the house and wondered what Kate would be doing.

Back at the house, while trawling through the brochures, 'Helping Hands' caught her eye. She rang the number. A woman named Brona answered, and explained that their organisation was made up of volunteers who helped the elderly with small household tasks such as, fixing lights, small plumbing jobs, and minor-garden chores. "However," she added, "your larger jobs, such as replacing doors and the clearing of the back-yard jungle, would be outside our realm." She gave Annie the phone number a man called Keron, saying his prices were reasonable and his work was good.

That night she spoke to Anthony on Skype. They each made a cup of tea and pretended they were sitting next to each other. They discussed her idea in regards to having Kate's, external glass, sliding door changed for a normal one. No matter how many times Annie explained that it needed to remain open in order to cause a draft for the fire, Kate would forget and close it again. The chimney sweep fellow told them it was imperative that the room had a draft to take the fumes away. It worried Annie, that with the winter looming, they would be breathing in smoke. Anthony agreed that she should ring Keron and get a quote.

The following morning Annie called in at the doctor's surgery with forms from the Social Welfare. They were to be signed by her, and for them to state Kate's medical condition. She then went to pick up Kate. When she arrived, Theresa's friend, Betty was there. Theresa offered a cup of tea, which Annie accepted. Kate was delighted to see Annie and greeted her as if it was the first time all over again. Annie explained to Theresa, that she and Kate would be going to Dundalk the following week, to catch up with a friend from Australia who was home on holidays. As they drove away, Kate touched the crucifix that hung from the rear view mirror, "This will keep us safe," she said. Annie reached across and touched her hand.

On returning to Spiddal Road, and on seeing the wall covered in photographs, Kate was in raptures, and during the evenings that followed, she would point to a certain picture and relate a story. Annie realized how the Alzheimer's had taken a firmer hold. Kate would point to a picture of her late husband Oliver, and say, "That is my father," or to one of her brothers, and say, "There is my son." This deterioration of her memory, deeply saddened Annie.

The next few days, for Annie and Kate, were filled with picnics, luncheons, and short drives to the outskirts of Dublin. After mass, on Sunday day morning, they went to the Phoenix Park for morning tea. The trees had begun changing colours and Kate commented on how beautiful they looked. They discussed a concert that Father John had mentioned. A local choir would be performing in the church on the following Thursday night and Annie had bought two tickets.

Chapter Ten

In, the afternoon when Theresa and Adrian arrived for Kate, Annie watched as Theresa scanned the room for changes. When Annie bent to fasten Kate's shoe, she noticed Theresa's feet and in particular her french-polished toenails. A wave of contempt washed over Annie. The toilet was broken and blocked with faeces, but Theresa had her toenails french-polished. Annie held her tongue but inside she was fuming. "Are you coming Annie?" Kate asked.

"No mam, I have to meet Brenda. She's invited me to dinner."

"That's nice," she said. Annie stood at the door and waved goodbye to Kate. Her emotions were mixed and the contempt she felt for Theresa was starting to poison her mind. She felt she needed to find herself again, and to stop reacting to her sister.

While at Brenda's, Annie was spoiled with food and laughter and subsequently persuaded to stay the night. Brenda and Annie had worked for the same insurance company in their younger days. Brenda now worked at a local school. After breakfast and after organizing Annie to lock up the house, Brenda left for work. "Don't you be lonely," she called back, "my door is always open."

After enjoying a hot shower Annie drove into the city. She loved the city streets, the smells, and the air. Dublin was her city. While there, she bought a sandwich and a coffee and took them to Stephen's Green. Stephen's Green was special. In her younger days she would sit there with Brenda and eat lunch. Today the park was full of travellers, mums with babies, toddlers throwing bread to the ducks, office workers, and the odd vagrant. She sat for a time, and people-watched.

Later she called at the curtain shop, and then on to the doctors, where she picked up the Social Welfare forms. On returning to Spiddal Road, she sat and read the forms. The doctor had filled in her part; however, she had written over the residential address that Annie had provided, and put Theresa's address instead. Annie wondered why she had done this. She made an appointment for the next morning.

Annie knew that if she didn't have the carer's pension, she would struggle financially, and taking on a job would defeat the purpose of being with Kate.

Later that evening she discussed her concerns with Anthony. Anthony voiced that he was upset at what was happening and suspected that Theresa was setting up the hurdles. The following morning Annie met with Kate's doctor. "My name is Annie Quinn," she said, "I'm Kate Murray's daughter. I left a form at reception, asking if you would fill it in; but you wrote my sisters address and not Spiddal Road Ballyfermot. I am applying for the carer's pension. I left Australia to care for my mother. The social welfare sent these forms for me to fill in, however, the address reads as if she is not living with me."

"But your mother lives with Theresa."

"How do you know that?"

"Theresa told me that she has been living with her for the past few years."

"It would appear that you have been fed a pack of lies," said Annie, "I live in Australia and when I ring my mother, I ring her at her home, which is Spiddal Road. Theresa took my mother to her house only recently, after I informed her I was coming home to care for her. Did Theresa also tell you that our mother has lived in squalor since her illness?"

"Look Annie, as far as I am concerned, your mother lives with Theresa and not you. I only see Theresa in this surgery, not you."

"Let me remind you Doctor, when I was home last year I discovered my mother had not seen a doctor for several years. I noticed her rubbing her knees, her tummy, eating Rennes, as if they were going out of fashion. I rang your office, if you remember. I asked if you would ring her and invite her to come in under the guise of a blood pressure test. If you cannot remember, I certainly can. We left your surgery with four referral letters, all written by yourself. It was I, Annie Quinn, in your surgery, not my sister. She had never before even noticed the things that our mother was silently suffering from." Annie then began to cry, and when the doctor insisted that she was not changing the address, Annie gathered up the form in frustration, and left.

Returning to Spiddal Road, she met the handy man. He took a look around the house, and commented that she had her work cut out for her. At this she burst into tears again. What happened with the doctor, had put her stay in Ireland in serious jeopardy. The handy man reassured her that it would all be okay. She apologised to him for her outburst and took his business card. She felt like she was fighting a major battle but didn't understand why. Liam called later and offered his services with a few jobs and she was grateful for his help. Kate could choose new curtains and rails, and if Liam dismantled the old pelmets, she could give the windows a new look.

That evening she did more painting and the following morning she accepted a quote, from the handy man, that included hanging the doors. She also arranged the pest control as well as a quote, from a local man, to clear the garden. Anthony had arrange a skip and would help with the clear out.

Later that afternoon she showed the local man the back garden. "Holy Shit! I've never seen such over-growth. There's no way I can tackle this job Missus. Everything would have to come out through the kitchen. My suggestion is that you find at least four men with chainsaws and maybe a mulcher."

The following day as she was driving to pick up Kate, she wondered what tricks would be waiting for her. Again Kate greeted her as if it was their first time. Theresa was a different kettle of fish. She had set the rules, she decided what days Kate would see Annie and what allowance Kate would have for her time with Annie. It appeared random, eighty euro's one week, sixty-five another. This point in particular annoyed Anthony. He pointed out to Annie, that Kate's pension came to almost three hundred Euros.

Annie asked Theresa why Kate didn't collect her own pension. At this, Theresa snarled, "She asked me to collect it for her, so that's what I do."

"But I'm here now; I can take her to collect it."

"I am collecting it! She asked me!"

"So," persisted Annie. "If you are collecting it, where is it?"

"I'm keeping it here."

"Why?" pressed Annie.

"Because I am, that's why."

"I need to buy curtains for the house."

"She doesn't need curtains."

"Theresa, they're falling off the wall with the filth. They're hanging in shreds." Theresa spun around to her mother and moving close up into her face, she growled,

"You don't need curtains, do you mam?" Kate looked terrified as she answered,

"No! No! I don't." Kate looked to Annie. "It's ok Annie, it's ok. I really don't need curtains." The fright on her mothers face, broke Annie's heart. Holding back the tears, she turned to Theresa.

"This is not right. I will have to seek advice. This is definitely not right." Theresa crossed her arms under her breasts and moved toward Annie, and with a smug knowing look, she snarled,

"You will never be able to do anything." Annie read in this comment, a veiled threat.

As they drove away from Theresa's, Annie explained to her mother that the bankcard had arrived, and that it would be necessary to use some of her money to buy curtains and to fix a few things around the house. She took Kate to the ATM and they withdrew the money required. Annie guessed that by the time Theresa had figured things out, the tradesmen would have been paid.

That night she rang Anthony and told him what had happened with the curtains, and also about Theresa's veiled threat. "Anthony, it was almost as if she was revealing something, cryptic-like. It's hard to explain, but she had a knowing look in her eyes. Anthony pondered a few seconds before he said,

"It sounds to me, like they have taken out a Power of attorney over mam"

"Anthony! There isn't a doctor in this land that would find our mother *compos mentis*. That would be insane. They could lose their licence over that.

"What else could it be? They've removed her from her house. They've taken her pension. What more could they want, but a power of attorney over the rest of her assets."

"Fuck," said Annie. "If they get enduring power of attorney, they'll have the right to say who she can and can't associate with. They could even stop us from seeing our own mother."

"You could find out the details from the Four Courts," concluded Anthony.

After they hung up, Anthony turned to Pam. "That was Annie," he said. "She was telling me how big sister bullied mam today. Also, after Annie suggested that mam needed new curtains, Theresa made a threatening remark to her. It was like, nah-nah nah-nah, I know something you don't know. I'll bet she's taken out Power of Attorney."

"Her arrogance galls me." replied Pam. Anthony again pondered.

"That's a lot of control," he continued, "and I'll bet good old Adrian is the puppet master."

It was raining lightly when Annie and Kate arose. Annie had prepared a picnic hamper to take on the train. They were going to Dundalk, to catch up with Annie's friend, Cathy. Kate became excited like a child on boarding the train and spoke with everyone who passed her. Annie was amused at the reactions of those who did not quite understand her problem, but it never embarrassed her.

Cathy had brought the sun out to greet their arrival in Dundalk, and the three women spent a wonderful day: First on the sea front watching the ocean, then lunch together and eventually a relaxing hour in a local pub. Overall, it was a successful day. After hugs, Kate and Annie boarded the return train. Cathy waved from the platform, as Annie mouthed through the window, 'see you in two weeks.'

On their arrival back in Ballyfermot, Annie reminded Kate of the church concert. "If you're too tired, we can give it a miss," she offered. Kate would have none of it, saying she was looking forward to seeing all her friends.

They had front row seats near where the altar had been transformed into a stage for the Gospel Choir. Annie was never again to see Kate as happy as she looked that night. She glowed as she rocked, swayed, and sang her heart out.

When the concert ended, Theresa turned up. She appeared nervous as she hugged Kate. "I was so worried about you," she said, while fiddling with Kate's neck scarf. "Your phone wasn't answering. Are you ok mum?

"We went to Dundalk," said Annie. "I told you last week we were going. If anything had gone wrong, I would have let you know." Theresa appeared close to tears.

***

The previous day, while sitting at his laptop, Anthony put a question to Pam, "What would you say if I were to send Theresa a strong message by email?"

"About what?"

"To be honest, I just can't stand her crap any more. She's stressing me, and God knows why she's giving Annie such a hard time. This should be a great opportunity for mam to have some quality time with family, and there's Theresa, hell bent on sabotaging everything. I've already written a draft," he said, while moving aside to let her see the computer screen. Pam took some time to absorb the content of the email, and then let out a deep sigh before answering.

"You remember what the doctor said about stress? This action could lead to another heart attack. You were lucky last year; the next time it could kill you, and that's not what your mother would want."

"What Theresa is doing is so wrong," he replied. "and that's what's stressing me. She needs to be stopped. If I don't tell her how I feel, I will definitely have a heart attack." Pam raised her hand towards the screen and replied, "Then press the send button."
'Theresa,

I am a man with faults who has done bad things in my life and sometimes I have done good things! I am your average Joe. I do however, truthfully know - I want what's best for my mother. But it's not all about what I want so I look to finding a consensus with my brother and two sisters. This works in most families because most families would get together and decide between them the likely future and what each member can bring to the table. I have seen it happen several times with other families. I am no angel as I say and I am deeply ashamed of my part in the fact that my mother lived like an animal in a mouse infested Shit-hole with blocked toilet and festering bed linen.

I am deeply ashamed that I took her off a train in Limerick without checking her living conditions in Dublin when I knew that her personal hygiene had lapsed due to her condition. Somehow - And I know that this does not absolve me of my responsibility - I never considered for a second the possibility that my mam could be living like that. But you knew it and you are responsible for your share of it. You even admitted seeing rotting dinners on her dining room table. But you would say things like "what about the pen and ink - She does my fucking head in- it's a break I need from her Why does she lie to me?" etc-etc. obviously not understanding that she has an illness and what you see are symptoms. I do know if I lived in Dublin it could not have happened and I am confident that would be true of my other siblings.

I can honestly say that I have never had a go at my Mams dignity and never shared your snide remarks about her! So it comes as a great concern to me that you have appointed yourself in charge of Mams

affairs. You got Mams pension signed over to your name only in July when you knew full well Annie was coming to live with and look after her sick mother. That was dishonest devious and sneaky. It was also taking advantage of a very vulnerable sick woman who could not have asked you to do this while understanding Annie was coming to help. How come you didn't tell us that? Were you ashamed of it? Did you know somewhere inside it was wrong? Or did you just forget.

And now that Annie is here to help look after mum don't you think it's appropriate that the pension go back to mum??? Particularly as you have to travel to Ballyfermot to collect it? And mam can't??? You are either stupid or dishonest?? When you did that you insulted me as well as your sister.

As recommended by Alzheimer's Society of Ireland and as agreed between you me and Thomas in June. The best place for Mam is her own home. We discussed home help together (Which we would pay for!). But when another sister offers to travel 10,000 miles to help her sick Mam in her own home - well the shutters come down. God forbid the thought of it! Now the only person - and I have told many (including the Alzheimer's Association) who think that this is a bad idea, is you! It seems to hurt your pride, to hell what everyone else thinks - it's your gig - and your sister

has not the right to care about her Mother. The last time I tried to reason with you I was told to "Fuck Off" and you hung up the phone!

So I'm not going to try again because you cannot be reasoned with!

You insisted Mam be with you three days a week - (I suspect when you figured how it would affect your sisters chance of getting a Carers Allowance.) You got that! You insist Adrian attends family meetings - Well you and Adrian can attend as many family meetings as you like but I will not be there! That's another insult! I have two sisters and one brother end of story. I have seen your recent texts to Annie where you talk about protecting Mams routine. Wake up and tell me a mother in the entire world - Alzheimer's or not - who would not love the thought of spending a week with her daughter returning from the other side of the world?

But again it's about you! And you honestly believe that a woman who started going to a social club some 2 1/2 weeks earlier had a routine?

May you one day wake up to the enormity of the situation you have created! I borrowed some money from Mam which you my brother and sister know about - but how much did Mams son in law charge for varnishing the door and painting the sills at Mams house? You never did tell. Mam costs us practically zero to put up? What's it now costing her now to stay with you??? You never did tell? I don't suppose her other children have the right to know? We should just trust you? Well we did that before and look what happened!

I still feel guilty over my part in Mams "shithole" ordeal and making her last days comfortable and happy are now a real option with a sister living with her. But your "Insane Jealousy" is stopping that! We should be doing everything to make this work - not scupper it! But it's clear you want Annie on the next available plane. This is quite obvious by your actions! You are not the head of the family for a few reasons I can think of (like the notion only exists in Mafia Films!) but mostly because you have wrecked your family! You do not deserve the respect that such a position might require if it truly existed.

Have you ever heard of equality? Well get with the program and stop listening to amateur legal eagles-Get yourself to a real solicitor and bring this email - He or she will put you right!

All this because a sister wanted to live with and take care of a sick mother! And you weren't in control! You've been fighting a war with whom exactly? Who demanded what? When? Just you! You are the only one making demands, trying to control, manipulating your vulnerable mother- "You don't need curtains do you Mam!!!" Mam needs a lot more than curtains and you still cannot see it!

Regarding Mams house - if it's not good enough for you and me - it's

not good enough for our mother! GET IT!

Your vision is blurred by your need to be at the centre of everything.

NOW HERE'S A DEMAND FROM ME! - You put Mam back in charge of HER LIFE. Give back the pension immediately and stand back......you have your three days (as demanded and granted) don't try to control the other four.....if you do then LET ME MAKE MYSELF CRYSTAL CLEAR - you WILL NOT be welcome here anymore and any relationship with the Limerick branch of your family will be IMPOSSIBLE! GET IT! BACK OFF! Or pay the PERMANENT consequences of YOUR actions!

If you know different reply (by email - NOT the phone! We've tried that)

- If not - don't bother!

IF IT'S NOT OUT IN THE OPEN - THEN IT'S NOT HONEST!

This has gone too far! No more power games! People are hurt and not

sleeping because of you!

What an utter shameful, embarrassing, stomach churning mess you have made of your family all created by your own obsessive behaviour!!!!! ....

Anthony

PS. I dare you to show this email to independently minded, decent people! Ask what they see?
- But you can't because they only have your version don't they? They don't have all the facts!

Theresa had at first stared at the email in shock, and then began to seethe in a somewhat confused anger. She rang Spiddal Road several times, while mouthing for Adrian's ears 'They're a pack of bastards,' and, 'I'll bet Annie put him up to It.' the frustration of 'no answer,' at the other end of the telephone, led her to drive to Ballyfermot with Adrian. On seeing all the cars outside the church, she remembered that Annie had been in Dundalk all day, and on going inside the church, she felt that Annie didn't act like she had knowledge of the email.

Ever since Oliver had died, Christmas had been an issue for Theresa. She had told Anthony and Thomas that Kate *did her head in*. She informed them that she would not be having Kate at Christmas anymore because she was an embarrassment in front of her freinds. Theresa set the status quo: One year Kate would go to Anthony and the next year she would go to Thomas. Pam had offered Annie and Kate a genuine invite this Christmas, but there was complete silence from Thomas. Annie felt that being with her grandchildren in Limerick would be a good tonic for Kate.

Liam called at Spiddal Road one night and chatted with Kate and Annie. He looked at the curtains and rails and decided on an evening to hang them. Anthony would be arriving on the following Sunday with Grace and Sean, and the skip had been ordered to arrive early on the Monday morning.

At Houston Station the children ran along the platform to greet Annie. From the station, they all went into the city, where they window shopped, went for tea, walked along the quay before crossing over the Liffey, on the Ha'Penny Bridge. The children loved Dublin, and Annie was delighted to share their company.

It was nearing the festival of Halloween and Liam was keeping everyone's spirits uplifted with his incessant humour.

They all knuckled down and attacked the considerable work, such as, taking down the old cupboards over the stairs, opening up the alcoves in Kate's bedroom and pulling up sections of miss-match carpet. In a short space of time the skip was full with everything except the wood.

As it was Halloween and several local kids, ranging from five to ten years old, turned up with a shopping trolley and took the scrap wood to make a bonfire at the ring across from Kate's house. Annie gave them a few trick-or-treat lolly bags, that herself and Grace had filled. One kid slapped another, across the back of the head, and was making him swap lollies. Annie called out, "leave him alone he's smaller than you."

"Ah, he's only a bollix," said the older boy, and with that a phone rang. To Annie's amusement the five year old took a mobile from his pocket.

"It's me ma," he announced, "I'll have to leg it." Annie laughed at the spectacle.

"Don't you just love 'em," she said. The kids dragged off enough wood to start two bonfires.

Anthony and Liam made an attempt at the jungle in the backyard, including chopping back some of the briers and making the coal bunker safer for Annie to collect the firing. Anthony suggested that if they were to wait till next February, the overgrowth would lose most of its foliage and there may not be so much to cut down. They all agreed that this was a good idea.
Their hard work finally paid off, and the house was looking much better for their efforts.

Anthony and the children were returning to Limerick on the Tuesday evening and Annie promised them, on their departure, that she would bring Kate for another visit.

When Annie called at Theresa's the following day, Theresa was all smiles. Annie at this stage had given up trying to make sense of her moods. That evening Liam screwed the rails and hung the first set of curtains to cover the dining room windows. Brenda and Annie painted the room a nice cream, which against the olive green curtains made the room look lovely. Kate looked so happy "When I sort out the lounge room mam," said Annie, "perhaps Liam will hang those curtains as well."

"No bother," he said, "just give me a shout when you're ready."

Then, just to add the finishing touch, Annie placed a vase of flowers on the table. At this gesture Kate became teary eyes.

"Oh, Annie you are a great girl. I love you."

"It's my pleasure," she said. "Now, wouldn't a nice cuppa just round the day off nicely?"

After mass the following morning, Annie and Kate headed for County Meath. Driving through the countryside was liberating for the two women. Liam had dubbed the pair, '*Thelma and Louise.*'

Annie saved every receipt, be it for lunch, petrol, or any other purchase. These she placed in a red biscuit tin.

While looking at the Christmas decorations for sale in one of the shops, Annie brought Kate's attention to a wreath. "We could dress it up mam," she said, "and hang it from the door."

"That would be really nice," she answered, with a smile. Annie figured that giving Kate a purpose, such as setting a table or chopping the veggies, would help to slow her deterioration. As a dementia nurse Annie had seen and learned so much over the years.

On the way home they stopped at the *Borza* and indulged in beer battered fish and chips, with fresh crusty bread and butter. "Sure it's a feast fit for a king," remarked Annie.

Monica Dunne phoned Annie and invited her out for a coffee. "But I can't leave mam alone," said Annie.

"Bring her to my parents; they'd love to catch up with her."

Kate stayed with Mrs. Dunne while Annie and Monica went to the Liffey Valley shopping centre for a coffee and a chat. Their conversation was mainly about the developing hostilities effecting Kate. Annie confided that she suspected Theresa and Adrian, of cooking up some kind of skulduggery. Monica told her that the neighbours were commenting on the improvements made to the house since her return home. "I'm not sure how long the progress will last," remarked Annie. "When Theresa finds out I have access to mum's account, she will hit the roof. I'm also trying to find someone to clear the garden. It needs doing for everyone's sake."

"Don't stress Annie, the neighbours are with you. We know you came home to be with your mum. It's a disgrace what Theresa is doing. I'm just sorry your family have had to endure her nonsense."

On Sunday morning Annie rang Theresa and arranged for her to pick up Kate at the Liffey Valley Shopping Centre. She felt that this neutral venue would prove amiable for all concerned, which it did. It also had the effect of keeping Theresa from seeing the work being undertaken on Spiddal Road, hence buying herself more time.

Anthony was to receive an award at a gathering in Dublin and had invited Annie to be his guest. Mary McAleese, the President of Ireland, headed the prestigious VIP list. Amongst the calibre of citizens invited, Annie felt a sense of personal shame, in the fact, that she had left Ireland. She felt a strong sense of loss, at the life and times she had not truly shared with her country folk. In spite of her misgivings, the night was wonderful. The old Union Hall, where the awards were held, had been refurbished by ex-prisoners. The man, who organised the employment of this, otherwise unemployable workforce, received an award for his initiative. The ex-prisoners themselves were informally recognised with a warm handshake from Mary McAleese. Annie was so pleased for these men. Mary McAleese gave a speech that recognised all the people on stage for their tireless work, saying, how their work radiated light into the world. She spoke of their opposites, meaning the people who can drain life, *radiators and drains* she called them. Annie liked her analogy.

Looking at Anthony on stage holding his award, she felt an

immense sense of pride. After the formalities, those gathered were invited to eat, drink, and mingle. The invited guests were also encouraged to ask the awardees' about their initiatives. Anthony and Annie found themselves in conversation with the ex convicts. "Why aren't you drinking?" asked Anthony.

"We were asked to abstain until everyone left," replied one.

"Would you like a drink?" he asked.

"Is the pope a Catholic?"

Annie in her heels, stood shoulder high to Anthony at the bar, as he ordered four pints of Guinness. They felt like ham actors, while trying to sneak out of the big hall unnoticed with a pint in each hand. The 'boyo's' were gratefully waiting with their tongue's hanging out, and with a renewed confidence, Annie clip clopped back to the bar to order two more pints. Annie and Anthony enjoyed their time with their new found drinking buddies. They talked with them on all manner of things. Annie spoke with a father and son team of reformed crooks. "We now do gardening and stuff," the son said with pride.

"I might just have a job for you," said Annie, while soliciting a mobile phone number.

Later that night, as Anthony and Annie walked toward their hotel; she announced her idea to commission the lads to clear Kate's jungle. 'Why not?" he said, "they might prove more trustworthy than some members of our own family."

Life was tough for Greg in Australia. He had vacated his home and put his life on hold while making numerous sacrifices for Annie. Because she was not eligible for the carer's pension, he would send her money when he could. Annie's finances were none the less strained. She was determined not to leech off of Kate. Anthony told her that giving Kate a good life was enough reason to share a few of her meals. "It's what mam would want for you," he added.

The pressure was starting to affect Annie's capacity to rationalise. One Sunday after Kate had left with Theresa, she felt a frightening anger well up inside her. She became incensed at the fact that they had removed Kate from her community, her church, her home, her friends and neighbours. Pacing the floor in a bid to burn off her anger, she told herself, not to allow them to change her nature. She opened her laptop and Googled the poem, 'The Lake Isle of Innisfree.' She read and reread it, until she had learned it by heart. *'And I shall have some peace there, for peace comes dropping slow'*... She decided, she would rise early the next morning and drive to County Sligo. Having never been to the *Lake Isle*, she felt in her heart that this was the right time.'

When Annie woke, the sun was shining. After packing a small overnight bag and some toiletries, she was in the car about to leave, when she remembered the biscuit tin containing the receipts. It would be her proof in case she was ever accused of stealing Kate's money. If the receipts were left in Ballyfermot, she feared Theresa or Adrian might destroy them. She ran back into the house picked up the tin and placed it on the passenger seat of the car.

During her journey, the countryside presented Ireland in all its glory. She sent a text message to Greg, letting him know she had taken off for a few days. Along the way she softened her mood by listening to classical music.

On approaching Sligo town, the sight of Benbulben, a plateaux type mountain, appeared on her distant right. Knocknarea another mountain landmark appeared to her left. After arriving in the town, she parked beside Sligo's imposing cathedral. On calling in at the tourist information office, a young lady assistant gave her a run-down on the sights, as well as printing for her a map of the district. On the map the assistant highlighted the places of most interest: Loch Gill with its Lake Isle of Innisfree, caught Annie's eye. There were several megalithic sites marked, as well as the burial place of the poet, William Butler Yeats.

Knocknarea, the one thousand and seventy foot limestone monolith, fascinated Annie, especially when the assistant mention that 'Maeve's, Neolithic burial Cairn' stands atop the summit.

Annie's latest granddaughter in Australia was born, a few months earlier, coincidently, on Annie's birthday, and she was named Maeve. For this reason alone, Annie pledged that she would later climb to the summit.

Loch Gill to the east of Sligo town was everything Annie imagined, and more. Parking her car beside a castle on the shore line she stood and looked for several minutes, in an effort to take it all in. A cruise boat had been moored nearby and a sign on it, read: 'Off season for day trips.' Annie felt so close, and yet, so far. She promised herself that she would return one day and stand on the Isle of her dreams.

She drove around the lake until she saw a sign directing her to Innisfree. The drive took her some kilometres along a boreen that twisted and turned before another sign read, 'Innisfree 2km.' she felt giddy when she reached a small empty parking area. She left the car and strolled past a cottage to where a pontoon lay moored at the edge of the lake. Standing at the lakes edge she felt a reverence as her eyes were drawn across the surface of the lakes low misty shroud, to rest at a point where the geographically small, yet spiritually powerful sight of the 'Lake Isle of Innisfree' held her enthralled. And for several minutes her tears ran freely and sweetly down over her face, as she stood amidst the sounds of small woodland creatures that mingled with the gentle lapping waters of the lake. She felt humble and yet, a firm and integral part of the moments greatness. Was this the *peace* that the poet had spoken of?

After returning to her car, she sat for several minutes trying to rationalise what she had experienced. It had been the strangest yet, most peaceful, moment in her life.

On leaving Loch Gill, new feelings and thoughts filled her with an invigorating strength and sense of goodness.

She secured a B&B near the town, bought a take away meal, and took it to a park bench where she consulted her tourist map. She decided she would attack the formidable 'Knocknarea' the following day.

It felt good to be awakened by the sound of traffic in Sligo. She found a café in the town and ate an ample breakfast. Feeling more alive than she had felt in weeks, she watched, as early morning diners entered the café, some bought take away coffees and some stayed for the big breakfast. She looks normal, Annie thought as she tried to pick out the people she thought might be care free. She wondered if these strangers thought the same of her.

It was still early so she went back to the B&B, lay on the bed, and checked for emails. Nothing appeared in her inbox. She lay on her back and stared at the ceiling. Where is it all going, and where will it end, she pondered. Thomas entered her thoughts.

Chapter Eleven
***

One year earlier in Ireland, she was out with her two brothers for a drink. The subject came around to their father, Oliver, and the hatred, the two boys claimed they held for him. Anthony related a memory of when he was a young lad. It seems something happened at school, and Oliver decided to confront the head Christian Brother. The argument had become heated, when the brother remarked to Oliver, 'I believe you are the most belligerent man I have ever come across.' At this remark, Oliver dragged Anthony by the hand and stormed out of the school. Once outside the school, Oliver asked Anthony, 'do you know what belligerent means?' Anthony had no idea. And as soon as they got home, Oliver looked the word up in the dictionary. They all laughed at Anthony's story. However the real shock for Annie came when Thomas announced that he not only hated Oliver, but Kate also.

"Oh my God!" said Annie. "I can't believe you just said that. Why do you hate our mother?"

"Because she didn't protect us. She could have kicked him out, or left him. I hate her because she did nothing."

"But," said Annie, "mam didn't have the capacity to deal with his tyranny. Like most women of her day, she just had to put up with her lot. It was the social conscience of the times."

Annie tried to sway Thomas, to see his mother's side of the situation.

As she pondered her current situation, she became more confused about why Thomas hadn't tried to contact her. Did he hate her as well? She loved Thomas. She remembered a large, tastefully furnished, room with a long wooden table. With nuns, talking to herself and her siblings. One nun asked Kate to go into an adjoining room and pick out one of the babies. Kate was taken aback at this suggestion, saying that it was impossible to choose one over the other. Compromising, she gave a blue and white outfit to the nun, while asking her to choose a baby boy. A few minutes later the nun returned carrying Thomas. The hood on his suit was too big for his tiny face. When Kate held him, she cried and immediately fell in love with him, as indeed did the whole family. Thomas was six weeks old.

Irish law at the time stated, that within six months of starting, the biological mother had to sign papers finalising the adoption. However, Thomas's biological mother had moved to England, and for almost two years, Kate worried that the mother might one day change her mind and ask for her baby back. Annie recalls Kate saying that Thomas was her son, and that she would go into hiding if they tried to take him away from her. She loved Thomas the same as she loved all her children. The woman was eventually found and, much to Kate's delight, the papers were signed.

Annie loved playing with her baby brother. She remembered with fondness her mum asking her to help feed him with mashed banana. He would smack his lips together as he savoured the taste. Years later, she and Thomas were travelling on a bus. Thomas was about ten. He was seated facing a lady passenger. "Annie," he said, pointing his finger at the lady, "that lady has a face like a pike." Annie was mortified at the time, yet, the memory has somehow become a happy one.

At twenty, Annie was married to Damien and they were living in their own home. She recalls that about this time, Oliver had been drinking heavily and in a fit of temper, had thrown Thomas against the fireplace, resulting in Thomas hitting his head. Kate was so distressed that she took Thomas to a neighbour for safety. Kate had no way of stopping Oliver. In one desperate moment she even asked the parish priest for his help. He advised her to go home to her husband. 'What God has put together,' he quoted, 'let no man pull asunder.' He added that, 'God will provide for his children.'

Thomas began taking refuge at Annie's. She had told him that their house was his. One of the bedrooms, which he occupied most weekends, was referred to as, 'Thomas's room.' This was how things went until, aged seventeen, he went to Cork and subsequently joined the navy. Annie understood his leaving. The image of her beautiful brother being thrown against the fireplace would haunt her, and she easily understood his reasons for turning his back on Dublin.

***

Chapter Twelve

Back in Sligo town, Annie threw her things into a bag, checked out of the B&B and headed for Knocknarea. Maeve's Cairn, looking like a large pimple on its top, would have been difficult to miss. She drove through the town and then westward towards Strand hill. The autumn weather was being kind to her, and as she approached Knocknarea, the wide asphalt road gradually gave way to a slow, narrow, and winding boreen. She felt lucky not to meet any oncoming traffic as the boreen led her up and around the base of the monolith to a gravel car park.

On leaving her car, a well beaten walking track allowed for little confusion as to the direction, and it was all upwards. Heavy dew on the grass and stones caused her to slip a couple of times. The early part of the ascent made her realise that she was not as fit as she should be, although, what she lacked in physical stamina was compensated for with a dogged determination to finish what she had started. She stopped several times during her ascent, to rest, and to admire the view. She smiled at the beauty of Sligo, as it lay out its ancient story filled landscape beneath her. Climbing higher and higher she felt a wonderful sense of freedom. Nearing the summit the incline eased, and her breathing became easier. There, ahead of her, unique in its scale and geography, stood Queen Maeve's resting place. Built, using millions of loose stones, during the Neolithic period and standing over thirty feet tall, the Cairn commanded a priceless view out over the larger part of County Sligo, including glorious west coastal views. Annie stopped and marvelled at the awesome extent of the cairns structure. Her imagination fired with thoughts of Maeve the warrior Queen, entombed standing up, and facing her old enemies to the east. Annie enjoyed the solitude and welcomed the detachment from what was happening in Dublin.

Leaving Sligo her heart again grew heavy, and her mind began to return to negative feelings: Enduring Power of Attorney, an image of Theresa, with folded arms, threatening, that she would be powerless against her plans. Annie made a mental note to go into The Four Courts in Dublin and educate herself on the questions she had surrounding 'Enduring Power of Attorney.'

Back in Ballyfermot, she Skyped Anthony telling him of her wonderful time in Sligo. After describing the feelings that had touched her at Innisfree, and how she had felt a strange and powerful peace there, he replied that she had found her *thin place*. "What's a thin place? she asked.

"It usually happens outdoors when you are feeling at one with nature. You may feel the sense of a place being holy or blessed. You may also feel a strong presence. It's called a 'thin place' because it's like a veil between you and the 'God of your understanding,' while in that particular place; you feel so close, it is *thin*.

"Wow! That is exactly how I felt."

The following morning, she took a bus into the city where she crossed the Liffey and walked the remaining distance to the Four Courts. The city made her think of her grandfather. He was the first person close to her that had passed away. She was nineteen at the time and remembers that she struggled to come to terms with his loss. The old city buildings were his spirit. She could hear his voice telling her, 'Annie look, up there at the bullet holes. Up there on the walls. They were put there, during the *Rising*, in nineteen sixteen."

After arriving at the Four Courts, she was directed, through a passageway, to the department she required. "How may I help you?" asked the young woman.

"My name is Annie Quinn," she announced, "and I'm inquiring about an Enduring Power of Attorney. I need to know if someone has taken one out on my mother."

"Sure, what's your mother's name and date of birth?" Annie supplied the information, and the girl searched her computer.

"No," she said. "There has not been an Enduring PA taken on her."

"Are you absolutely sure?" pressed Annie.

"It would be on this screen," replied the young woman.

"Could it be in someone's basket, waiting to be processed?" Annie persisted.

"It doesn't work like that," she said. "If one is brought here, then it is immediately put on the system."

"So," said Annie, "as of today, there is no Enduring Power of Attorney over Catherine Murray's affairs, and neither is there one in the pipeline?"

"That is correct!"

"Thank you so much."

Annie rang Anthony. "I have just left the Four Courts, and there is no EPA."

'Thank God for that," he said.

"Can you imagine?" said Annie. "Theresa, with that kind of power. She would have the say on whom mam could or could not associate with. They've practically stopped me seeing mam. And that's without an EPA. It's too scary to think about. I'm sorry for going on Anthony, and I do feel much better for getting this clarification. There isn't a doctor in this land," she continued, "that would find our mother compos mentis, especially after being diagnosed with Alzheimer's for so long. Her mind is too far gone to even understand what an EPA is. I myself had to read and reread the detail to get the full meaning of it. Anyhow Bro. It's been a great day and I'm looking forward to Christmas with you all.

Annie picked up Kate and they drove to the local supermarket for supplies. The following morning they set out on their train journey to meet up with Cathy and her family in Waterford. Annie had prepared a few sandwiches and cakes to sustain them, as they chugged along. Cathy had hired a cottage in Waterford and she invited both Kate and Annie to stay overnight. Annie could see that anything out of the ordinary might cause Kate some upset, so she declined this offer. They had lunch with Cathy and spent a few hours in Waterford before heading back.

Kate smiled at the countryside as it passed her by. Annie had parked the Katemobile' at the train station in Dublin. Their day was topped off nicely when they stopped and enjoyed a nice meal of fish and chips. Annie loved to see Kate happy. She loved the thought of them both making memories. Knowing that Alzheimer's would rob Kate of her 'family memories,' was a constant worry to Annie.

Kate stayed in bed the following morning so Annie decided it might be a good day to paint. Preparing the doors and skirting's with masking tape, was her least favourite job. When Kate did rise for the day, Annie seated her by the fire and made her eggs on toast. Kate appeared settled and happy in herself, so Annie began applying the undercoat. The doors were previously a dark brown and with just the undercoat applied, they were looking a lot more cheerful. At one stage Kate dragged a chair over and sat near Annie. "That's very nice Annie; it looks grand."

"It's just the undercoat, mam. When I put the finishing coat on, I reckon it will look wonderful."

"Thank you Annie. No one does anything for me."

'Mam, you don't have to thank me. It's my pleasure. Yesterday was a great day in Waterford, don't you think so mam?"

"Waterford?" said Kate, with a blank look that showed no conception of the reference.

"Ah, sure it's a great place ma. I'll take you there one day."

"I'd like that," she said, "I love the country." At that moment the phone rang and Kate picked up the receiver, "Hello. Who? Annie? Annie held out her hand and Kate passed her the phone.

The caller was Margaret O Callaghan, Kate's advocate. She was ringing to make an appointment to interview both Annie and Kate at their home. After some deliberation, the appointment was arranged for the following Wednesday. During this conversation, Annie explained that Theresa had set the rules and she was to pick Kate up after day-care. "We will be back in Ballyfermot at 4:00 pm" she said, "so I'll see you then."

After mass the following morning Annie and Kate went to order the blinds for the front windows. That same day Keron made arrangements to hang the doors. Liam also came and unblocked the toilet; although, happy that he had, Annie still felt embarrassed for asking him. While he was there, he rang his brother Seamus. Seamus spoke to Annie and arranged to pop around with Liam, on the following night.

Having the boys visit was a tonic. They laughed and reminisced with Kate. Seamus checked out the kitchen walls and told Annie that he would love to hang the new wall paper. "Thank you, I really appreciate that" she said, "but I really need to have the back garden cleared first, the reason being, the foliage has to be taken through the kitchen and it would scrape the wallpaper."

"Fair enough," he said, "just ring me and I'll be pleased to help in any way I can."   "Thanks Seamus, you're a star," Annie said, as she hugged the boys' goodbye.

Kate's spirits were high after her nephews left. "Two lovely young men. They were very nice," she said.

As Annie and Kate sat by the fire, the wall of memories again became the topic of conversation: "There's my father," Kate said, while pointing to Oliver. "And there's my son," she added, while pointing to one of her brothers.

After mass the following day they went to the Phoenix Park for morning tea. The tree's had lost most of their leaves, and had begun to hint at the approaching winter.

Annie would set the fire each morning so that it would be ready to light when she returned home with Kate.

With Theresa and Adrian coming to collect Kate, Sunday had become a part of the week that was a downer for Annie. 'If they really cared for her,' she rationalised, 'wouldn't you think they'd be happy that she was in her own home? Surely they should be happy that she's getting out and about and enjoying what bit of life she has left?'

As soon as Theresa and Adrian arrived inside the house,

Theresa made an excuse, on the pretext of looking for Kate's spare glasses, to go upstairs. Annie knew full well that she just wanted to see what changes had been made. When she came back down, she said, "Come on mam? We're taking you home."

"Are you coming Annie?" Kate asked.

"Sorry mam. I need to finish the painting. But thanks anyway. I'll see you on Wednesday." As Annie waved her mother goodbye, she felt a foreboding. Slumping on the chair she dropped her head into her hands, but then immediately stood back up and forced herself to snap out of it. She went upstairs and into the musty roof-space to locate the Christmas tree, while there, she saw reminders of a childhood, these included, dust covered toys, and things the boys had made at school. Back downstairs she picked a place that would best show off the Christmas tree. The decorating of the tree, with tinsel and baubles, she thought, might be a nice activity for Kate, on her return.

Meanwhile at Dodder Valley, Kate was seated in front of the television and Theresa had begun telling Adrian what she had seen upstairs in Kate's house. "Someone must have helped her," she said. "The carpets are all pulled up, the cupboards that dad built and that linen cupboard over the staircase, gone. There is no way Annie could have done all that by herself. Who could she be getting in? The fucking cheek of her, having people in that house."

"It's interesting all right," remarked Adrian. I wonder where the money is coming from? Has her bank statement for last month arrived yet?

"No it hasn't. Far out! Do you think Annie got the money out of the bank?"

"Ring them tomorrow," said Adrian, "and see where the statements are being sent. If the address was changed, then perhaps it's time to up the ante. What would you say if we were to speak with Mejella?" Adrian added. Theresa smiled,

"Fuck it! Let's do it," she said.

Back at Spiddal Road, exhausted from painting, Annie fell into bed around 2:00 am. The following morning after breakfast she took a stroll along some of the streets of her childhood. She met a woman called Martina. As a child Martina had been a neighbour on Spiddal Road. Martina's mother also suffered from Alzheimer's. The two women stood and exchanged teary eyed stories. Martina told Annie that her brother had moved back home when their mother became ill and that he did everything for her. When she was hospitalised, he extended his care to include other patients with dementia. He was so capable at what he did, the staff would sometimes ask him to come in and deal with their more awkward patients. Annie was so moved, by this wonderful story, that she bought a bunch of flowers and called at his house with them. There was no one home so she asked his neighbour to give them to him. In an appropriate card she wrote a short message praising him for his humanity, and suggested that the world needed more people like him.

Arriving back home, Annie finished the top coat of paint on the kitchen door. While standing back to admire her work, she hoped that Kate would approve.

Later that day on Skype, Annie walked the laptop around the house, a couple of times, to show both Anthony and Greg how the work was progressing. The positive comments she received, from family and neighbours proved a great source of fuel for her.

Lying in bed she began thinking about the next day and the day after. She hadn't envisaged when she made the decision to come back to Ireland, that she would be spending so much time alone. She never realised either that money, particularly the lack of it, would prove such an issue. Greg tried his best to keep her afloat.

Window shopping became a serious hobby, and she spent more and more of her spare time looking in the city shops. Dublin from Annie's eyes had seen a lot of changes. She walked along a boardwalk, that had recently been built, on the inside walls of the river Liffey. 'Jesus!' she said, to herself, 'they've turned the whole place inside-out.' She bought a coffee and a sandwich and headed along Grafton Street to Stephens Green. Even though it was a cold day, the park was alive with mums pushing strollers, pensioners feeding the ducks, and the occasional tourist. Annie loved it. She felt a sense of belonging in Dublin. After people-watching for a while, she drifted back into more window shopping.

Browsing through the fashion stores, within the shopping centre, she decided that she preferred the look of the winter clothes. The manikins had been dressed in smart woollen coats and scarf's, women's boots and hats. While in the store, she tried on several hats before conceding that she didn't look good in a hat.

On her way home, she sat upstairs on the bus and thought about the following day. 'Keron would hang the French doors, and Margaret would arrive at four for their prearranged talk.' She got off at the shops and bought a few slices of ham for the visitors. Thoughts of the new doors excited her. The room was going to look so much better and the fireplace would at last work efficiently.

Back in the house she closed the old sliding door for the last time, watched some television and then wearily climbed the stairs to her bed. It was a bitter cold night, and so she put the last blanket on the bed and crawled inside, she pondered how Kate must have suffered through all those long winter nights.

When morning came she dressed, rekindled the fire, ate breakfast, and made the house presentable for the day ahead.

Right on time the doorbell rang. "This is Sam," said Keron, "he build you doors." Annie extended her handshake to both men.

"Welcome. Come in. Would you like a cup of tea before you start?"

"Thank you," said Keron, "I have other job. Sam, he likes tea. I will call back later; see how the doors are working."

Sam told Annie of his life in Poland, and how it was getting harder to find work. Annie enjoyed his stories and she told him of her life in Australia. He was surprised and amused that kangaroos were commonplace on her property.

She received a text from Theresa: *Don't come at three o'clock, we are going out for the day. Come between 7 and 8.*

She stared at the message. 'Well, what do you know?' she thought to herself. 'They must be taking mam to Galway or somewhere for the day. It's about time they did something nice for her.'

Annie didn't dwell on the message, choosing instead to believe they were heading out socially. She remembered that Margaret had made an appointment for 4pm, so she phoned her.

"Hi Margaret, its Annie, just to let you know that mam will not be here today as planned. I just received a message, and I am picking her up tonight instead."

"That's no worries. Can I still come and have a chat with you? It might be better, that your mum is not there."

"I'll have the kettle on," said Annie.

The day passed quickly, as she fussed around, while spoiling Sam with sandwiches and biscuits. Margaret arrived, just in time, to see Sam upend his toolbox, which sent dozens of nails onto the floor. The three of them helped to pick them up. Keron arrived at this point and it was agreed the job was grand. Keron told her that he would call back for payment later in the week.

The boys eventually left, and Margaret and Annie's began a conversation, that covered all manner of things, including the photographs on the 'wall of memories.' Margaret asked Annie about each of her siblings in turn, she said she wanted to get an idea of their characters and traits. Thomas was the first photo in line, Anthony was second, Theresa third, with Annie last. Annie had calculated this order so as not to put Theresa first. She now smiled at the order. It amused her to think that Theresa might one day come into the room and rearrange the photos.

Annie explained to Margaret how she loved her brothers, and how it made her sad that Thomas was being cold with her. She explained how Oliver told people in front of Thomas, often tactlessly, that he was their adopted son. Annie reinforced that she was at a loss as to why all of a sudden Thomas had become aloof with her, especially since a short time earlier, he and his family had spent a wonderful time holidaying with her in Australia. She told Margaret how Thomas had declared only one year earlier, that he hated Kate, and how his revelation had shocked her.

She moved on to Anthony, explaining that he was married to Pam, and how they shared two lovely children. "Anthony was always the brainy one," she said, and continued, to proudly boast, how he had received an award from the President of Ireland for his initiative on a Third World Project. "Anthony," she added, "has declared his disgust at Theresa's behaviour, towards both me and Kate." She added that even though he 'gets down' emotionally, he still manages to maintain a wicked sense of humour. Annie took a deep breath before pointing to Theresa. "And her-self!" she said, as her adrenalin began pumping, "she thinks she is different to the rest of us. As children, it was as though we, that is, Anthony, Thomas, and I, were one distinct group and she had been cut from a different cloth. Theresa would treat me and the boys as her subordinates. She thought she was deserving of better than the rest of us. Thomas was good at taking the piss out of her." Annie continued, saying that Theresa was self centred, and had no patience, and nothing was ever her fault. Annie then looked at her own photo. "That just leaves me," she said. "I feel I was the peacemaker and the clown. I never liked fighting and I tried hard to make it all OK. Children don't really have a handle on some things, and I guess I internalised all the bad stuff. I'm not blaming my parents, but I sometimes feel I didn't reach my full potential. When I met Damien at the age of sixteen, I was looking for a way out. I married young, and probably did so for the wrong reasons. I love my parents dearly; but then I upped and went to Australia? Am I guilty of leaving them? Did it make me less of a daughter? That's how two of my siblings are making me feel."

Margaret was supportive in reassuring Annie, that we all make life choices, "It's what life is all about," she said. "Coming home to help your mother showed that you cared. For whatever reason two of your siblings don't want you here; you are not in control of that."

The conversation moved on to the condition of the house and the grants that Kate could have had. Annie felt comforted that Margaret was looking out for Kate. They hugged goodbye, with Annie saying that she would drop in to her office with Kate for a further chat.

Chapter Thirteen

Come between seven and eight, Theresa's text message had read. Annie decided she would arrive at eight, so as to avoid being left on the doorstep for an hour.

Before leaving Spiddal Road, Annie checked out the french doors, and hung the welcome wreath on the main door. The Christmas tree and the decorations stood waiting. The thoughts of herself and Kate decorating the tree later that evening made her feel very happy. Little did she know, at the point in time, that fate had other plans: The Christmas tree would never get dressed, Kate, would never enjoy her French doors; not even for one night. Annie stoked the fire and put the screen in front of it.

While pulling the front door closed, a sprig of holly fell from the wreath. She reattached it and made a mental note that it needed a few more decorations.

Adrian's car was parked in his driveway when Annie arrived for Kate. 'Ah well, they're back. At least I won't have to wait outside in the cold,' she thought, as she pressed the doorbell. Two or three long minutes had passed when she rang the doorbell again. Adrian opened the door and she stepped inside. Kate was lying on one lounge, and Theresa was laid on the other covered with a blanket, as if unwell. In a strange tone of voice, Kate asked Annie, "What do you want?"

"I've come to take you home." The fire is blazing and the house is warm," said Annie.

"I don't go with you. I stay here. I live here now. Theresa is very good to me. She gives me all my dinners. She is the only one that looks after me. She says, I can stay here."

Kate's body language looked strange, her eyes were wide, and her voice was monotone. It struck Annie that her words had been rehearsed.

"Mam, it's ok. Let's go home?"

'I am not going with you!" With that, Adrian jumped up, and

pointing at Annie, he boomed out.

"Your mother's wishes have been heard. She does not want you to have anything to do with her affairs. We are looking after your mother. Not you!" Annie began shaking. In her peripheral vision, she saw a woman coming out of an adjoining dimly lit room. The woman held a notebook and pen in her hand and was looking at her.

"Who are you?" asked Annie.

"I'm Mejella," she answered. Annie tried to compute the name Mejella?

"You are Theresa's police officer friend?"

"Yes I am," she replied. With that, Annie looked first to Kate, who looked stressed, then to Theresa, who was hiding under the blanket, and then lastly to Adrian, who had an expression like the proverbial, 'cat that had caught the mouse.'

"I can see what's happening here," said Annie, while looking at Mejella. "You were brought here to witness my mother's refusal to come with me. You knew she was going to refuse. This is a set up. That's why you were hiding in the darkness. You're here to intimidate me." Looking hard to where Theresa was peeping from under the blanket, Annie fought back her tears and continued, "You Theresa are a disgusting excuse for a human being." Theresa had postured, as if to speak, when Mejella stooped down and advised her to say nothing. Annie invited Mejella to step outside to where she might speak to her without upsetting Kate. Mejella refused.

Having said her piece, Annie gave Kate a goodbye kiss, and then left.

On the pavement she thought she was going to faint. Inside the car she cried so hard that she drove onto the footpath and turned right instead of left. Realising she was in shock; she pulled over and stopped the car.

A thousand questions ran through her head. 'Why did Kate pick tonight to refuse to come? Was it a coincidence that a Garda officer was in the shadows with a note book? God, what are they doing?'

She phoned Anthony's house and Pam answered. Pam told Annie that Anthony was on his way home from college. Annie broke down and told Pam what had just taken place. "You are joking? Anthony will be livid. I won't tell him while he's driving but I'll get him to ring you the minute he comes in. Ring Liam. Don't be alone tonight Annie. I realise how hurt you are, and I'm feeling for you."

'I'll be OK," she said, trying to sound brave, "It's just that they keep hitting me these blows, and I can never see them coming. I actually imagined that they had taken mam out on a day trip.

After speaking with Pam, Annie composed herself and drove home. The Christmas tree that had promised so much fun, now sat wanting, in the corner of the room, like a sad metaphor for Annie's struggle.

Annie was stoking the fire when her phone rang. "Jesus Annie, the woman is mad!" said Anthony. "What she's doing borders on the criminal. Take yourself down to the Garda station in Ballyfermot and report what happened. This friend Mejella had no right to be using her position as Garda officer, in this way." Annie began to cry.

"Anthony, how did it come to this? Wouldn't you think that Theresa would be pleased that mam had the chance of happiness in her own house? I'm at a loss as to how this is happening."

Outside the Garda station, Annie's phone rang. It was Thomas. "Annie, Anthony just told me what happened. Jesus, that's terrible. I'm so sorry. She shouldn't have done that."

"Thomas, when is it going to stop? She's keeps doing crazy stuff and I think Adrian is behind it."

"I'm not sure what to say," he answered. "Take care, Annie," he said, before ending their brief exchange.

At the Garda Station Annie gave a brief explanation of what

had happened. "I'm sorry," said the officer, "but we don't get involved in domestic disputes." In frustration, Annie raised her voice a tone.

"But that's my point. There is a Garda officer involved." She was directed to wait in an adjoining room. A female officer joined Annie and began asking questions and taking notes. Annie could tell by the tone of the questions and answers that she was being given the run around. She left the station frustrated. She sent Anthony a text, explaining her experience, and then drove home.

That night as she climbed into bed, she felt cold, stressed, and disillusioned.

Throughout that same night Anthony was unable to sleep. He paced the floor, drank coffee, and racked his brain. At 4:00 am he Googled the Garda Ombudsman. He had started filling in the questionnaire when he stopped to read the warning about fraudulent complaints. He continued and added more information. After reading yet another warning, he took a breath and pressed the send button. His complaint, on Annie's behalf, basically, accused a Garda Officer of entrapment and intimidation.

Annie awoke the next morning and was unsure of what to do next. She knew that she would never set foot inside Theresa's house again. Margaret O'Callaghan popped into Annie's mind. She dressed and made her way to the Citizen's Advice Office. She was a half an hour early so she went upstairs to the canteen.

The events of the previous night ran through her mind: Her mother's face, Theresa under the blanket, Adrian roaring, "*Your mother's wishes have been heard.*" She began to weep and as she did the entire canteen bore witness to her inconsolable sadness. She remembers the kindness of a stranger who held her.

As Annie descended the stairs, with her eyes red and swollen from crying, Margaret O'Callaghan appeared outside her office. "My goodness what's wrong?" she asked, while indicating to her receptionist to make coffee. At this point Anthony phoned and asked if he could speak with Margaret. A three way conversation ensued and Anthony explained that he had lodged an official complaint with the Ombudsman. Margaret then asked if they wanted her to make a referral to the *Elder Abuse Officer*, in relation to the matter. She qualified that the Elder Abuse Officer, was a new position created by the government, when it realised that this type of abuse was becoming rampant in Ireland. Elderly people were being targeted, mainly by family members, in their bid to get at easy money. Both Anthony and Annie agreed that Theresa and Adrian should be reported. They voiced their belief that Kate was being bullied, and that her basic human rights were being denied.

Margaret began to type a letter to, Joan Mc Hugh the Elder Abuse Officer for south west Dublin. Margaret explained to Annie that Joan Mc Hugh had a large area under her watch, and that it may take a while for her to get in touch. Almost two hours had passed by the time Annie left Margaret's office. The two women hugged as Margaret assured her that something would be done.

'Where did all those tears come from?' Annie felt emotionally drained and yet, consoled that at last someone might be listening. Her next thought was about the shit hitting the fan when Theresa realised she had a bank card.

Annie went to the ATM to get the money to make the final payment owing on the blinds. The money for Keron was in an envelope, waiting for him after he made the final adjustments on the costing of the doors. Annie inserted the card in the ATM and it was DENIED. She tried again. DENIED. She drove back to the house. Inside she looked at the bare Christmas tree and it felt like the soul had been ripped from the house. Opening the cupboard she placed the bank card, alongside the receipts in the biscuit tin. She started a fire; having had plenty of experience doing this in their farmhouse back in Australia, only there she often used pine cones and rolled up newspaper.

It was late afternoon. She had never, to this point, feared her own company but she felt it now. She reflected on the promise she made to her mother. It had been a naïve, if not selfish promise, that had not factored in what her siblings might have wanted. She questioned if she was a good daughter. She berated herself for not being stronger in standing up to Theresa. She then rationalised that such an action would have placed Kate in the middle of a bigger dirtier battle. She worried about her finances. Every thought she had was negative.

Tiring of the negativity, she decided to use her time productively, if for no other reason but to occupy her mind. She opened a small cupboard underneath the stairs. It was originally created by Oliver, to house the brooms and such likes, and was currently filled with general rubbish, including mice nests and a disgusting amount of their droppings. She started once more to feel resentment toward Theresa and Adrian. She began to verbalise her frustration. "Fucking bastards, fucking bastards.

She Skyped Anthony and learned that he had received an email from the Ombudsman saying they would investigate. Anthony's opinion was that Mejella could face disciplinary action for her part in the so called 'domestic'. Annie reminded him of the parable in the bible where two women both declared that they were the mother of a particular baby. King Solomon could not decide which was the true mother, so he declared that the child be chopped in two, and each women given half. One woman yelled out 'No,' let her keep the child. Solomon knew then that she was the true mother. Annie did not want any harm to come to Kate, and had made a decision that she would no longer play the tug of war. Anthony agreed and suggested that they leave it in the hands of the Elder Abuse Officer and the Ombudsman. "What are your plans?" Anthony asked.

"I could just stick my tail between my legs and head back to Australia," she answered, "but Greg has paid for his trip to join me for my fiftieth birthday, and besides, I don't want to give Theresa that power. There are things I can do that don't cost money and I will still visit mam in the day-care centre. Perhaps I can become a volunteer and spend my time with her?"

"That's a good idea Annie, but don't be stuck for anything, you can call Pam and myself, anytime."

"Thanks bro. I love you."

"Love you too sis. Talk tomorrow."

'*Annie, Annie, please come to me,*' Kate called out. Annie was about to swing her leg out of the bed, when she realised that she had been dreaming.

Over the next couple of weeks Annie found it so hard at Spiddal Road without Kate. Her friends Clara and Brenda had each shown care by inviting her to stay with them at their homes, and in spite of not wanting to impose, she did find herself accepting their kindness on a couple of occasions

As the days dragged by, she felt more and more alone. Her heart sank when Mr Dunne told her that he had met Theresa and Kate at the local shops that morning. The shops were only five minutes walk away.

Annie met a friend (Marian,) for lunch. As fate would have it, she told Annie that a friend of hers was working in the new day-care centre. She told Annie how to get there, which picked her spirits up, no end. After they said their goodbyes, Annie wandered through the shopping centre. She needed to be amongst people, amongst the paradox of a community of strangers.

The following morning, while following the directions to the day-care-centre, she wondered if Theresa might have warned the staff not to let her see or to take Kate away. She would never take her away. She knew Kate was in their care, but until she got word from The Elder Abuse Officer she didn't know what the rules were. She decided to take it easy until things were sorted. Both she and Anthony had debated this, and both felt they had to leave it in their hands.

Unsure where the entry to the day-care centre was, Annie went into a foyer of the building only to find a supermarket. Going back outside, she looked up, to see Kate's distinctive white hair, and her salmon pink cardigan. Kate was sitting at a table, next to a second floor window. Tears welled in Annie's eyes. A man was coming out of a small doorway and she asked him how she might get up there. He told her to ring the bell and talk through the intercom, which she did, and a friendly voice directed her to push the door open and take the lift. As she came out of the lift, Kate was walking past with the aid of a walking stick, "Mam," said Annie, in a quiet voice. Kate turned and immediately lit up.

"Oh, sweetheart. Dear God, It's you Annie. Oh thank you God. It's Annie, its Annie." Dropping her stick, Kate hugged Annie like she hadn't seen her in years. Annie went with her to the ladies room, and when they came out, Kate began telling everyone that her daughter Annie, had come to take her home. Annie encouraged Kate to sit down at the big table and to introduce her to her friends.

After a spending couple of hours together, a care worker came and announced that the bus was ready to collect the first lot of people. As Kate struggled, Annie helped her on with her coat.

"You're going in the second bus," the care worker said.

"It's ok," said Kate, "I'm going home with my daughter; she's come to collect me."

"No mam," said Annie. "I can't take you today. But I will soon; I promise."

"But where are you going? Why can't I come?"

"Sorry mam, but I have a few things to do. I'm trying to fix up the house. It'll be OK. I'll come back." Annie felt so bad having to deny her. She would have loved to pack her into the Katemobile, drive off into the country, let her see the trees and the shapes in the clouds, then take her home and listen to more stories from 'the wall of memories. Annie wanted more than anything in the world to be with her, but she knew she had to walk away.

Later that day Annie had her first panic attack. She felt strangely uneasy, giddy even, and not sure what was happening. Depression was becoming a regular companion and she had increasing difficultly being alone. Anthony understood the signs and after speaking to her at length he convinced her to come to Limerick.

The following day she began her drive to Limerick. As she reached the outskirts of the town, her phone buzzed. Adrian's name appeared and his message read, "*Your mother does not want to be with you for Christmas.*" Annie began to shake with the images of them brow beating Kate. Anthony had received the same message.

Chapter Fourteen

When Annie arrived in Limerick, Pam expressed her anger at Theresa's behaviour. She was infuriated with the text message. Then later, without saying a word, Pam took the phone to an upstairs bedroom and rang Theresa. Theresa saw that the incoming call was from Limerick and handed the phone to Adrian, "Hello," he said, while pressing the speaker button."

"Its Pam. May I speak with Theresa?'

"She may not want to speak with you," he answered, bluntly.

"Why would that be? Did I do something wrong to her? Theresa indicated to Adrian that she would take the call.

"Hi."

"Theresa, what on earth is all this about? and why is Kate not coming to us for Christmas?"

"She doesn't want to be with Annie."

"What do you mean; she doesn't want to be with Annie? She loves being with Annie. We've seen them and they're great together."

"She's angry with Annie, for wrecking her house, stealing her money, and giving away her fur coats.'

"You are disgusting Theresa; do you know that?"

"I am not," Theresa barked, in a bid to defend herself. Slowly and clearly Pam reemphasised.

"You Theresa are the most disgusting woman I have ever met." With that Pam slammed down the phone and returned down stairs, while grasping at her chest and shaking. "I need time out," she said. "I need to be alone," She picked up her car keys and left the house.

Annie turned to Anthony, "How is this going to end? Our sister is mad. She's mad and she has our mother captive."

"It's fucked,' declared Anthony, while holding his head in his hands.

"I hate to say this Anthony, but I think it has a lot to do with finances. Mam's bank statements don't appear to tally." Anthony looked at Annie in surprise,

'Do you have mam's statements?

'Yes, I took her to the bank, a while ago. They're upstairs in my suitcase. I'll get them."

Annie returned with the paperwork and handed it to Anthony. Within seconds, he smiled a wry smile "Well, what do you know?" he said, "It looks like the McGee's decided, over Christmas dinner, not to lodge anymore of mam's pension into the bank. Look down this column? Since December of last year, there are no lodgements." Annie had arrived at the same conclusion some time before, but had been wary of playing the 'devil's advocate'. "Well, let's include our brother in this." Anthony continued. "Perhaps it's time he witnessed a little more of our sister's activities. I'll email the statements and include a short message."

The following morning on finding the email, Thomas drove the three hours to Dublin. Theresa's was surprised, as he was the last person she'd expected that day. "Mam is at day care," she announced. "She'll be home at 3pm.'

"It's you I have come to see," he said, holding the email in his hand.

Later that afternoon, Thomas rang Anthony and was anything but friendly. "I have just left Theresa's, and all I can say is that you and Annie are sick bastards. You think that Theresa is ripping our mother off; when all along she is holding receipts for all mam's needs." Having made his unsubstantiated statement, Thomas then refused to discuss the matter further. Anthony put the phone down, turned to Annie, and said,

"She has receipts; so there you go… receipts!"

"For what?" Annie asked, with a look of bewilderment.

"Well, not for plumbing, rent, electricity gas, pest control, home maintenance, certainly not for gardening, telephone bills and food; mam has enough clothes to dress the population of Spiddal Rd, so not for clothing, coal or travel expenses." Anthony stared at

Annie. "Thomas has driven all the way to Dublin, and now he believes her."

"Did he sight the receipts?" Annie asked.

"He didn't say. My goodness," said Anthony, with a pondering sigh, "the plot thickens."

Christmas was looming and Annie told herself that she needed to move upbeat and try to capture a bit of her old spirit. A shopping trip to Limerick with Pam was arranged. She confided to Anthony that she planned to buy the children a telescope. He tried to convince her that it was an expense she didn't need. Undeterred Annie rang and asked Greg to send her money for Christmas. Christmas dinner in Limerick was to be hosted by Pam's sister. It would be an extended family affair, with family members contributing selected food dishes.

On Christmas Eve Annie joined Anthony and the children for midnight mass. Pam, who was terrified that she might slip on the ice, opted to wait out the service inside the car. Later, after the children went to bed, Annie, Anthony and Pam, sat up into the early hours, talking and drinking wine. They each expressed a sadness that Kate was not with them, and marked the occasion with a toast to her good health.

On Christmas morning Annie watched, with delight, as the children tore open their presents. When the telescope appeared from its wrapping, she wasn't sure who was the more excited, Anthony, or the kids.

Later, after dressing in their finery, they all arrived at the family gathering. Annie received a warm welcome from the in-laws and as the celebrations progressed, her thoughts never strayed far from Kate. She wondered what she might be doing, was she happy, and did she understand why they couldn't be with her.

There is a tradition upheld on Saint Stephens day in Ireland, It's called the 'WREN.' Musicians travel around the town and the outlying farms playing music and collecting money for the less fortunate of the community. Anthony, who had been a regular fundraiser for many years, invited Annie to take part in the 'WREN'. Her job was to open all the farm gates and doors to allow the minstrels access. Farming families would be sitting around their kitchens waiting to extend a warm welcome. Food and drinks were usually laid out for the musicians, so as to wet their whistles. Travelling around in the van and listening to the sounds of guitars, bodhran's and fiddles, gave Annie a great high. It was also her job to collect the donations. After visiting the farms they spilled into the town, and in particular, the public houses. People were most generous and their donations raised a sizeable amount of money. Annie had not felt this happy in a long time.

Shortly after Christmas, she received a phone call from Kavanagh's about collecting the blinds. She explained that she would pick them up early in the new year and the shopkeeper reassured her that, that would be fine.

Over the next couple of weeks, while Pam and Anthony were out working she busied herself, with ironing, laundry, and preparing the evening meals. During this period she rang the office of the Ombudsman to see if anything had happened in regard to Mejella, but ironically, nobody could speak to her, because she was not the official complainant. She rang the office of The Elder Abuse Officer and was told that her case worker had gone off to England, due to her father being taken ill.

Anthony's home is located in a small village. Annie would take walks around the country roads there. On one of these walks she came upon an old *estate house* that had recently been converted into a nursing home. 'Cahermoyle House,' as it was called, had once belonged to William Smith O'Brien, a founder member of The Young Irelander's. The grounds of Cahermoyle were stunning.

After returning to Anthony's house, she phoned the nursing home and enquired about a job. She was invited to drop her resume in, for consideration. Over dinner that evening, she spoke of her excitement at the prospect of working in Ireland. Later she received a call saying that they were impressed with what they had read in her resume. In particular, all her experience. They told her that they might be in a position to offer her work. However, she would first be required to complete a short course on manual handling and OH & S, Irish standards, as her Australian standard was not recognised in Ireland. She assured the caller that she would follow it up.

Chapter Fifteen

She phoned Greg and discussed the possibility of her working in Ireland, as well as the general details of his arrival the following month.

After hugs and goodbyes to Anthony's family, she left Limerick and headed across country to be with Brenda, in Dublin. While crossing the midlands, heavy snowfalls made driving conditions treacherous. At one stage, visibility became so poor, that she feared for her safety. But after a tense few hours she arrived, safe and sound to a warm welcome. "The room is yours anytime you need it," Brenda reassured her.

During a break in the weather Brenda and Annie headed for Kavanagh's to pick up the window blinds. On the way, they called at the Civic Centre. Annie asked the receptionist to give the biscuit tin filled with the receipts and the bank card, to Margaret. She also asked that it be held in their safe for, good keeping.

After Kavanagh's, they pulled up outside Kate's house in Spiddal Road, Annie felt sad. Inside the house, Brenda admired the french doors which Annie had wanted to paint but didn't get the chance. The Christmas tree, sad and bare, in the corner of the room, signified the futility and heart break of Annie's dealings with her sister.

Annie and Brenda hung the blinds and stood back to admire them. They stepped outside the house and the blinds looked equally impressive. The house was beginning to take shape. But that's where it ended.

Two days later, Brenda asked Annie if she would go back with her to Kavanagh's, as she wanted to buy curtains for her own house. While there, Annie met a neighbour who lived on Spiddal Road. The neighbour told her that Theresa had knocked on hers, and other doors the previous day, enquiring if they had seen anybody hanging blinds inside Kate's house.

Annie enrolled in one of the work courses, which cost more

than she could afford and she was forced to ask Greg for yet more money. The course went over two days and she loved every minute of it. She loved walking through the streets of Dublin on the way to her classes. She learned several things on the course, including manual handling techniques that would prove very useful. Her friends in Dublin were delighted to see her and told her that she looked better now, than when she lived in Dublin.

On a visit to see Kate, she felt that one of the workers steered away from her, in an unfriendly manner. Kate tried once again to leave with her. Annie told her that soon she would return and take her too Anthony's. She felt it was a white lie that had been necessary. Kate seemed satisfied and it made things easier when it was time to say goodbye.

The second course in Dublin was not available for a few weeks so Annie returned to Limerick. She enjoyed helping her niece and nephew with their homework. While bonding, they spent many hours, doing all manner of things. Annie imparted some of her imagination, such as showing them how to take photos of the trees while lying on their backs. Robert loved the shapes and angles, and he was keen to point out to Annie what he thought would make a good photo. Annie's phone rang. "Joan Mc Hugh," the voice said. "I'm the Elder Abuse Officer from south west Dublin. I was wondering if we might meet up for a chat. I have been to see your mother and I need to talk with you. I believe you are staying in Limerick?"

"Yes," Annie replied, "but I don't mind driving to Dublin."

Joan Mc Hugh had also phoned Anthony, asking his opinion as to the problem. Anthony filled her in on some of the home truths, and asked if she had ever seen a movie called, '*What ever happened to Baby Jane,*' where Bette Davis plays the part of a women who is insanely jealous of her younger sister. "In my opinion," said Anthony, "Theresa is insanely jealous of the relationship that exists between Annie and Kate."

Cherry Orchard Hospital was originally built to handle an

outbreak of Tuberculosis, and, with small buildings everywhere, it was like a rabbit warren, fortunately, Joan had given Annie instructions where to park.

She met Annie outside the office block and gave her a warm welcoming handshake. "Would you like a coffee?" she asked.

"That would be nice, but may I use your loo first?"

"It's the door on the left along the corridor." When Annie returned, Joan had hot cup of coffee was waiting.

"How was your trip?" Joan asked, during relaxing small talk. Annie explained that she loved being back in Ireland, especially driving through the countryside.

"Annie, would you like to make a start on the serious stuff, or would you rather I began?"

"You go ahead," said Annie.

"Firstly," said Joan, "let me apologise for the delay. My father took ill in England, and has subsequently died. I went to see your mum in Theresa's house. I was made most welcomed, and Theresa and her husband were very polite. Your mum looked well. She was smartly dressed with her hair kempt, and there was absolutely no evidence of physical abuse." Joan went on to say that she had told Theresa that having Kate living in her home was not an ownership thing and that Theresa's front door was now Kate's front door. Kate was entitled to have anyone she liked visit her, whether they are family or friends. Joan went on to say that she spoke of Kate's health and the importance of access to transparency in all aspects of Kate's care, and with all of her siblings.

Annie allowed Joan to speak without interruption until she herself was invited to reply. Annie looked into Joan's eyes and began to speak softly and assuredly. "Thank you for inviting me here today," she said, "I am truly sorry at the loss of your father. And thank you for the time you have taken to see my mother. Firstly, let me assure you that neither Anthony nor I, ever suggested that Theresa was a physical threat to our mother." Annie paused for a moment, and then continued. "I was raised in this part of Ballyfermot. This hospital, with its chimney visible from Spiddal Road, was part of the landscape of my childhood. I was one of four children. An average kid. Our father Oliver Murray was an alcoholic. He was abusive to our mother and also to his children. At the peak of his alcoholism he would turf us out onto the streets late at night. We often walked into the city, when we should have been sleeping in our beds." Annie leaned forward to emphasise her next statements. "So you see Maura, I am so glad that you found not a bruise on my mother. My father never left one bruise on my body either, but I'll tell you for nothing, that he fucked plenty with my head." Joan's eyes opened wide and her expression showed that she knew exactly where Annie was coming from. "So," continued Annie, "I really don't feel warm and fuzzy because she is now with my sister. I'm sure you know that there are many forms of abuse. I have witnessed my sister and her husband, emotionally abuse my mother. They stopped her from exercising her basic human right, to make choices and decisions. I saw my sister raise her voice to my mother, and I watched in horror as my mother responded, like a frightened child, the same way she did when my father ruled her,. Margaret O'Callaghan referred this matter to you after an event, whereby my sister, her husband, and their Garda friend performed an act of intimidation and bullying on me. It was nothing short of entrapment. Anthony and I need someone to listen to us. The Garda say it's a domestic, and don't want to get involved." Annie placed bank statements on the desk. "And what of her money?" she asked. "Where did it go? Her pension was passed over to Theresa, so where is it being spent?" Joan picked up the statements and began to read them. "It doesn't take a maths expert to work it out," said Annie, "Just look down this year's credit column and compare it to last year's?"

"May I hang onto these?" asked Joan.

"Of course."

Joan then asked Annie, why they didn't have a family meeting. Annie explained that they were going to have one. But when Theresa, insisted that Adrian be present, Anthony objected. He asserted that Kate had four adult children and they should be capable of making decisions on Kate's future, Annie agreed with Anthony's assertion and added that Adrian should have stepped back and allowed the siblings to make the decisions required for Kate's future well being. In reaction, Adrian arrogantly declared that he was going to be there boots and all. Anthony was adamant that he would not be attending any meeting that Adrian attended.

Joan responded, "If this happened in my family, I would say that there was no reason for all the in laws to be there. However, if it meant not having a meeting, even if the matters regarding my mother needed to be discussed, I would relent and allow the meeting to go ahead."

"Joan, after what Adrian has done to our mother and me, I am telling you, Anthony would flatten him. It's my opinion, that if a meeting, that included Adrian, ever did take place, Theresa would be nothing more than a proxy for him. He is without doubt, the ring master."

"It's a pity," said Joan, "because if such a meeting did happen I would be present, and I would observe which one took the floor, and I would then see the power play." Annie shook her head,

"It's not going to happen."

"What if I arranged a meeting between yourself and Theresa, here in my office? It would be on neutral ground and she would not be able to intimidate you on my patch." Joan's suggestion filled Annie with abhorrence.

"Joan," she replied, "these are not my words, but I am going to use them: My sister is a 'vexation to my spirit.'"

"The 'Desiderata," said Joan.

"Yes," replied Annie, "powerful words. Theresa and Adrian have disrespected me, violated my being, tried to destroy my very soul, and you ask me to sit with them and have a chat over a cup of coffee."

Again Joan's eyes showed that she understood exactly where

Annie was coming from, and smiled a sympathetic smile in acknowledgment of her anguish.

"Relax Annie," she said softly, "there will be no meeting with your sister. But its ok. We will work out a solution." Joan again mentioned the word ownership and tried to reinforce that Theresa did not own Kate.

"Yes she does," snapped Annie.

"Annie," said Joan, firmly, "nobody owns another. Your sister does not own your mother."

"Ah but she does," said Annie, with equal weight. Without saying another word Joan stared at Annie with an enquiring look. Annie softened her voice, "I know Joan that no one owns another, and you also know that no one owns another. But Theresa doesn't know that. As far as she is concerned, and as far as her behaviour is showing, she owns my mother. She tells her what to do, where to go, and holds her back from her family and friends, as and when she thinks fit. Neither God nor man can tell Theresa otherwise."

The conversation moved to Thomas and his lack of show. The two women had spoken for almost two hours when Joan said, "Annie this must be very hard on you?" This compassionate line became the trigger for Annie to let go the tears.

"It's extremely hard," she said. "Like nothing I have ever known."

"I am so sorry this is happening Annie. I promise I will continue to keep an eye on Kate's well being." They shook hands and for a moment Annie felt that Joan wanted to hug her; but maybe that would have been unprofessional.

Walking back toward her car Annie felt that she had made a breakthrough; someone else had heard her story. Surely what Theresa and Adrian were doing was immoral, if not criminal. Maybe under the watchful eye of Joan, Kate might enjoy more freedom to be with her family.

Driving away, Annie's mind went over and over the discussion she had just had with Joan. She could not bring herself to go to Spiddal Road, so she drove to Brenda's. The night was cold and she was handed a small gift of a hot water bottle, covered with a furry bear. The two friends sat cuddling their warm bottles and drinking tea into the night. Annie told Brenda of the despair she had felt while living on Spiddal Road. She opened up and talked about her thoughts of self harm: Speeding along country roads with thoughts of hitting a tree, or starving herself in an attempt to put a stop to Theresa's madness. She had read Mahatma Ghandi for inspiration, dwelling on how to stop craziness by quietly starving. "It sounds almost funny to hear myself telling you," said Annie, but when I was alone in Kate's house, I was in a very dark place. Brenda had started to seriously worry for Annie, but then Annie moved onto a lighter note, while explaining that her trips to Limerick had been her salvation. Brenda relaxed a little at this assurance and told Annie, that she was always there for her.

The following morning Annie said goodbye to Brenda and drove to the day care centre. Once again Kate was excited on seeing her. "This is my daughter Annie. She came all this way for me." Kate tried to put on her coat. "I'll come with you now," she said.

"Mam, I can't take you now, I have business to take care of. How about, in a short time, I will take you to Limerick for a holiday." Kate turned to the ladies sitting at the nearby table, "I'm going to Limerick on my holidays." Annie was consumed with sadness. She just wanted to say out loud to the whole room. 'She's my mother, and because my sister is a mad bastard, and she is stopping her from having a life, I'm taking her away. Annie kissed Kate goodbye and drove to Limerick alone.

She received a call from Cahermoyle House, asking if she had completed the courses required.

She had undertaken the manual handling, but the next course was not available for a few weeks. With Greg's visit nearing, she didn't think it fair to take on the job and then have to say that she wouldn't be working for a month while her husband was in

Ireland. She decided at that moment, with some sadness, to let the whole idea of working in Ireland go. She thanked them for their interest in her and said if ever things changed in the future she would contact them again.

Anthony and Annie discussed bringing Kate to Limerick for the Easter break. It was agreed that Anthony should send Theresa the request from his phone. The text told Theresa, that Kate would be picked up from the day-care on the Monday, and that she would be returned there on the following Monday. The text went on to say, that if Theresa had a problem with this, she should phone Joan Mc Hugh, as she has been advised that Kate needs to be allowed time with her grandchildren and family in Limerick.

Anthony sent the text and four hours Theresa's reply simply read, *'that's fine.'*

Chapter Sixteen

Brenda's mother in law had died after a recent illness and Annie accepted a request to house-sit, while the family travelled to England for the funeral. As Annie was returning to Dublin to pick up Kate, she decided it would suit for them both to stay at Brenda's. The chance of a break from Spiddal Road, proved irresistible.

When Annie arrived, Brenda's household was abuzz with the arrangements for their journey to England. A party of twenty people were heading over for the funeral. It was a huge show of support, not only by family members, but also, friends and co-workers. They shared a family dinner that night and Annie was given keys and instructions that included pets and their needs.

After Brenda's family left for the airport, Annie took a bus ride into the city. The buskers were out in force and going from one to another she took her time to listen, before continuing along Grafton Street. She was amazed at the talent. However during her walk she also felt the pangs of loneliness return.

The following morning she arrived at the day care centre. "Oh Annie! My lovely Annie. Thank you God. Thank you for sending my Annie."

"Your Katemobile awaits you," said Annie. "We're going on holidays." The staff wished them a good time, but Annie wondered what they really thought. She felt sure that Theresa would have fed them all manner of negative misinformation about her.

But now was not about negativity; now was about being free to enjoy precious time together. "These will keep us safe," said Kate, while touching the beads that hung from the rear view mirror. "I can see a baby in the clouds," Kate said, with the excitement of a child. Annie smiled and took her hand.

"I love you mam. I love you so very much."

"I love you too Annie."

It had been a while since mother and daughter had enjoyed tea and cakes in the park.

On their arrival at Brenda's, Kate became confused. Annie explained that they were just minding the house for a few days. At bed time Annie left the toilet light on and shared a room with Kate. Before sleeping she listened as Kate whispered a prayer for each of her children. This experience, for Annie, proved bitter sweet. To Kate, they were all her children and she loved them unconditionally.

After a somewhat restless night she drove Kate to mass. It was Shrove Tuesday, and again Kate's friends all asked, where she had been, and expressed how much she had been missed. Kate sat at the seat where Oliver's plaque was. She skimmed her hand across the metal. "This is my husband," she said, and began to cry. Again she left her seat to greet people that were coming back down the aisle from communion. Annie watched their faces; some were handling it well, while others appeared confused or shocked. Annie fought her tears. It appeared as though Kate was so pleased to be back, that she became overwhelmed and confused by her own actions.

The mass ended with Father John inviting the congregation to partake in pancakes and tea.

A short while later, he came and joined them. "Kate, I'm so pleased to see you back with us. " Annie it is also nice to see you again. How are you?" Kate interrupted,

"I live in Dodder Valley Estate. This is my daughter Annie," she said. Annie stood to one side and smiled at how happy Kate looked amongst all her friends. Father John asked again,

"Is everything ok Annie?"

"I don't know where to begin Father. Look at her. Look how happy she is. But looks can be deceiving. To be honest, it's all a big mess." Father John turned to Kate.

"Kate, you go off with your friends and have some pancakes, I need to speak with Annie. "Stand over here Annie and tell me what's wrong." Annie tried to keep it brief. She explained the promise, she had made, to come home if her mother ever became sick. She told him of the deception and intimidation, and how the entrapment, using Theresa's Garda friend, had become 'the straw that broke the camel's back.' Annie took a breath before continuing. "Father, being a man of God, it must follow that you believe in forgiveness. It bothers me greatly to say," she continued, "that I cannot find it in my heart to forgive Theresa."

"Let me give you my spin on forgiveness Annie. I do believe in forgiveness. I believe that if someone has made a terrible mistake and is absolutely sorry for that mistake, then we should forgive them. But this is not what is happening with your sister. She is showing no remorse and she continues to make a conscience decision to do more and more to upset Kate and yourself. Maybe you don't have to forgive this behaviour; not as long as she continues to do these terrible things."

"My goodness!" remarked Annie. "That has to be the best confession I ever made. Thank you, father." Father John and Annie joined the others.

Annie was happy to sit back and watch Kate flit around like a celebrity. She began to realise how popular she was, and how she was held in such high esteem by her community. When asked, where she wanted to go next, Kate answered with enthusiasm. "To the country."

Some years prior, one of Annie's friends had been killed in a car crash. When back in Ireland Annie would usually make the journey to County Meath, to pay her respects. She asked Kate if it was ok for them to go and visit. Kate agreed.

On their arrival, the graveyard itself was very peaceful. Annie's friend, Mary, had been buried along-side her husband. He had died five months earlier. They were both in their twenties.

Annie felt incredibly sad that Kate had no recollection of those memories. The graveyard surroundings, including the church and the thatched priests residence were beautiful. Kate asked Annie, "Do you think the church is unlocked, I would like to see inside?"

"Let's go and see mam. I would like to go inside myself.
After sitting in the church in silence, Annie and Kate spent time taking in the atmosphere of the beautiful church grounds.

Before leaving the church grounds, Kate again asked, "Do you think the church is unlocked, I'd like to see inside?" Annie could see that her mother had absolutely no recollection of, only twenty minutes earlier, sitting inside the very same church. Annie smiled as she replied,

"I'm sure it's open mam. I think I'd like to take a look myself."

On the drive back to Brenda's house, Annie detoured to sample 'Burdocks', *the best fish and chips in Ireland*.

The following morning herself and Kate travelled to Limerick. Anthony and his family were so pleased to have them back again. It was school holidays, and Annie, Kate and the children went off on a drive to Dingle. Whilst going over the mountain, they got lost. Annie convinced them that there really was no such thing as lost. "Look at the beautiful hills we are driving over," she said, "If we had gone the way we should have, we would not have had near as much fun." Sean looked at Grace,

"We're lost," he said dryly." They all burst out laughing. Annie took photos of Kate with her grandchildren as they all smiled and huddled together on the beach at Inch. It was a beautiful moment. They finally arrived in Dingle and had a wonderful time.

Arriving back in Limerick, Annie' received a text message from Greg, '*Hi honey, are you near your laptop. Skype me, I need to tell you something.*'

Chapter Seventeen

Greg sounded chirpy as Skype produced his image on Annie's laptop. 'Hello honey. How are things? How is your mum? Is she well? I'll bet she's happy to be with you all."

"Yes," replied Annie, "she's having a great time with Anthony and his family. She loves the kids. We've just arrived back from Kerry. We had a fantastic day. So, what did you want to talk about?"

"Your car has shit it self! I was driving to the farm and it just stopped outside Bathurst. I was stuck so I made an executive decision and bought you a brand new car."

"I hope you did not," she remarked angrily.

"Annie, listen to me? I was stuck. I had no choice."

"How much was this car?"

"Thirty eight grand. I put ten grand down as a deposit. We can pay off the rest over seven years."

"We now have a seven year car loan?" Annie's heart sank. "Fuck, fuck! This is all I needed; another nail in my coffin. Why didn't you talk to me first?"

"How could I contact you, when you don't answer your phone? I had no choice!"

"Don't give me that shit. You could have hired a car, called a taxi, rang your sister, stayed in a hotel, and caught a train home. Do not, fucking tell me, that you didn't have choices? You chose to do all this without any consultation. You made that choice. You knew that I would never agree to a car loan, so you just cut me out of the equation. Fuck you! Like I'm not under enough pressure over here. How's your maths Greg: I have lost one of my jobs in Australia, I'll be going back to less money, and I now have a seven year car loan. The conversation ended with Greg being frustrated by Annie's lack of enthusiasm for his purchase, and with Annie sitting on the bedroom floor weeping.

'Seven years with less work, and added financial pressure.'

The more she thought about it, the more her tears turned to anger. She wanted to scream, but instead she kept it inside. Something shifted inside her. It was now two weeks before Greg was due in Ireland and she felt seriously resentful towards him. She busied herself around the house while trying to distract her mind. The children were wonderful. She helped them with their homework and taxied them to and from their sports. It was a great opportunity for her to get to know them better.

Though Anthony and Annie had always got along well, she now saw a side to him that worried her. The work situation in Ireland had become dire and he was in real danger of losing his job. She watched him pace the floor. After a worrisome time, he had his contract of employment looked at and it was found that what his boss was doing was not correct. He ended up getting a reprieve from redundancy, but it came with a large pay cut.

Annie and Anthony would often go for a light drink at the pub or sit up into the small hours of the morning discussing their evolving family matters. Annie declared that if ever they made a movie about 'Kate's story,' she would like Helen Mirren to play her part. She asked Anthony who he would like to play his character. "Danny de Vito," he answered. They both laughed.

"Anthony Hopkins," said Annie.

"Why him?"

"Because," said Annie, "he's articulate, smart, and seems a lovely man." After pondering their parts, Annie asked, "who should play Theresa?'

"Shrek," returned Anthony, with a laugh.

"Nah," said Annie, "Shrek's too cute."

Annie arrived just as the plane had landed. She had mixed feelings about Greg's arrival. Part of her wanted to be hugged, and part of her felt betrayed. She went over all the good things he had done and tried to minimise his reckless actions. But this latest burden had been yet another lesson in forgiveness. She realised she fell a long way short on the virtue of forgiveness.

Chapter Eighteen

Greg had come through the gates, but as he walked on the inside of the barrier that divided them she didn't feel the 'rush'. Clearing the bars he looked at her with the kind of 'puppy dog eyes' that begged forgiveness. "Hi," he said, and waited for her reaction. She smiled, but didn't beam. He hugged her, but she didn't warm.

"I'll show you my $500 car," she said, unable to resist the sarcasm.

Driving towards Brenda's they chatted on the events surrounding Kate. "We'll be staying in Templeogue with Bill and Brenda, as I feel my failure in Ballyfermot."

"It's not your fault, you were stopped. You had good intentions, but Theresa and Adrian had other intentions. Stop beating yourself up."

On the way to Brenda's they called at the day-care-centre. Kate was delighted to see Greg. She cried and hugged him. The staff made tea and sat Greg, Kate and Annie together, at a small table, away from the others.

Annie had explained to Greg that she was trying to do the right thing with the day-care centre, but once again, it became upsetting for all concerned when Kate tried to put on her coat and leave with them. "This is disgraceful," said Greg. "If it was my mother I wouldn't give a fuck what anyone said. I would just take her."

"It's not that simple," said Annie, "you just can't walk in and take her. She is under their care and that means that they're responsible for her. I don't know what the exact rules are. I just don't want to do anything that might go against me. I have to treasure the bit of time I have with her." Greg had just witnessed the' rock and the hard place.' Leaving Kate was painful but taking her against the rules was far too serious.

Back in Limerick they discussed the possibility of taking Kate to Australia on holidays. "If we got her on a plane and sent Theresa a message, saying *she is safe*, do you think that would be kidnapping?" asked Annie.

"If she goes on a holiday willingly, and with her daughter, no court in this land would call it kidnap," Anthony added.

Greg and Annie took off for a few days. They travelled to Sligo, where Annie showed him Loch Gill and Innisfree. They climbed Knocknarea and spent time driving along the dramatic coastline of Mayo. She tried hard to fight off the resentment she was feeling towards him. Her thin place in Sligo had thickened and as much as she tried, things between them were not the same.

Annie's 50th birthday was looming. Anthony and Pam had arranged, with the local publican, for sandwiches and a birthday-cake to be supplied for a small get-together on the Saturday night. Through Anthony, Annie had got to know a few of the locals, and the invitations went out by word of mouth. The night proceeded very well and at closing time a 'lock in' was agreed and, in the Irish spirit of things, the traditional musicians played the party into the small hours. Annie enjoyed her birthday night immensely.

On the following Monday morning Annie drove to Dublin. She had brought with her a chocolate cake, and was excited at the prospect of sharing it with Kate and her friends. "I'm sorry," said one of the care workers, "your mum's not here today. Your sister phoned to say she wouldn't be coming in." Annie felt weak. Why would Theresa do this? Why would she be so vindictive? Annie figured that Theresa had guessed she would be coming to share her birthday with Kate. Annie stood in the car park teary eyed. She tried to contact Joan Mc Hugh by phone.

"Sorry," said a female voice, "Joan has left this position and has gone to another department. May I help you?"

"No, thank you," sobbed Annie.

Anthony was right when he spoke about civil servants. 'They can't get too involved, as they move positions so often, with their cases being passed on to someone else.' This was a serious blow to Annie and she felt as though she was back at square one. There was no one to watch Theresa. There was no official, looking out for Kate's interests.

Annie returned to Limerick, where Greg was waiting to continue their trip. Whilst their relationship remained strained, paradoxically she loved the thought of seeing more of Ireland with him. On their travels they stopped off in County Offaly to enjoy a reunion with old friends, Mona and John. Their hosts took them to visit Clonmacnoise, a sixth century monastery, situated on the banks of the river Shannon, in County Offaly. They strolled around the sacred place, while marvelling at high crosses, a tall tower, and many amazing stone carvings.

After leaving there, they wet their whistles, in a local pub. They were challenged to a game of pool by a couple of locals. The friendliness of the people in the bar became a pleasant memory for both Annie and Greg. That evening in their friend's home, John and Greg sat in the lounge room discussing all manner of subjects, while Annie and Mona sat at the kitchen table talking recipes and going over old times. At about 10.30 pm Annie's phone rang. "Annie Quinn?" asked a man's voice.

"Yes."

"This is Constable John Sweeney. I'm sorry to ring you at this late hour, but I'm on nightshift. I'm investigating a complaint made by an Anthony Murray, on your behalf. Would it be possible for me to meet with you in person?"

"When?"

"Is there anyway you might drop into the station tonight

"What station?"

"Templeogue."

"Well," said Annie, "I'm staying with friends in Edenderry."

"I could drive to you," said the officer

"How about I meet you at a station in-between?" suggested Annie. "What about Lucan Garda Station?"

"Perfect," he answered. "I'll ring and tell the sergeant to have a room available in one hour's time."

"Grand! See you then." Annie hung up the phone.

"Would you like some company?" asked Mona.

"That would be nice." Greg looked at Annie, with surprise.

"You're going at this hour?"

"Yes Dear!" she replied, with an air of condescension. "You're in Ireland. Don't wait up.

On her arrival at the Garda Station, she was introduced to a Constable John Sweeney. "Thank you for coming out on such an awful night, and at such short notice," he said. He appeared nice enough, yet Annie detected caution in his voice. He opened the conversation by announcing that he was given, through the Ombudsman, the charge of a complaint against a Garda officer. He then, without elaborating on the details of the complaint, asked Annie to give her account of what had happened during the night in question. This was easy for Annie, as it was as clear in her mind as if it had been yesterday. When she finished, he asked her, "What would you say if I told you, Mejella was not a Garda officer on that night?" His question threw her train of thought.

"I don't understand," she replied. He continued,

"She may not have been Garda that night. I have spoken with her. I am not at liberty to disclose certain things with you, but I feel she may not have been a Garda Officer." Annie shifted in her seat.

"Now I'm really confused! If you spoke with Mejella that indicates she is in the Garda. I don't even know her surname. All I know her by, is her Christian name, Mejella. I'm at a loss as to what you're getting at."

"Was she in uniform?" he asked.

"No," Annie replied. "But when I asked her who she was, she said her name was Mejella. I then said to her, you are Theresa's Garda friend, aren't you? To which she replied, yes. As far as I was concerned, I was in the presence of a Garda officer and I believed she was there for the purpose of intimidating me. If she wasn't a Garda officer, then she was imitating a Garda officer. I invited her to step outside so I could speak privately with her, and she refused." Constable Sweeney sat back in his chair.

"Annie, this is difficult. I am going to be the devil's advocate here. What if, and I am not saying that there is any truth in this, but what if your sister asked her friend to come over in case there might be a disturbance. Her mad sister had arrived home from Australia and was on her way to cause trouble at her house that night?" Annie looked back at him puzzled.

"I guess," she said, "Theresa can say almost anything she wants, and I'm guessing there will always be those who will listen to her. All I know for fact is, that at the time in question, I received a text message saying, '*Come between 7 and 8pm.* When I arrived, according to instructions, I was left standing for several minutes at the front door. When I entered the house my mother refused to leave with me. She spoke to me robotically and appeared to be doing so under duress, as if the words had been scripted for her. No sooner had my mother's refusal been spoken, when Mejella made her appearance from an adjoining darkened room carrying a note pad and pen. Entrapment, that's what I believed it to be. I still believe that the whole scene was stage managed in an attempt at entrapment. Unfortunately, it's only my word."

Constable Sweeney wound up the discussion by saying that he would look into the matter further. Then as Annie was rising to leave, he asked, "When are you returning to Australia?"

"My husband is here on holiday. I have decided to return with him on the twentieth of the month."

"OK," said the Constable. "I hope to be in touch with you again. Thank you for your time Annie."

Chapter Nineteen

Greg and Annie said goodbye to Mona and John before heading back to Ballyfermot.

Annie had promised Mr and Mrs Dunne that she would tackle the clean up in the back garden but it never got done. On seeing the mess Greg remarked, "Holy shit!" Annie was thinking of naming the garden, '*holy shit.*' "I have never seen such a messed up garden. This is incredible!" he added.

"I told you Greg, but until you see it for yourself, it's hard to imagine. My dad always kept it neatly mown. I saw an image on Google Earth, dated a few years back, and it was like this then. If my mother had fallen, I dread to think of her injuries. Where were Theresa Adrian and their two strong boys?"

"This is a huge job," said Greg. "At least the foliage is bare at this time of year. How about we pick up some serious gardening tools and come back tomorrow?"

Strolling around the house, Annie tried to go up-beat, by showing off the paintwork and general clean-up that had been accomplished, but the Christmas tree, standing sad and bare, said it all. "Do you want me to take the tree down?" he asked.

"Nah." said Annie. "Leave it for Theresa, she can read into it what she will. She'll most likely see it as a symbol of my defeat. '*You will never be able to do anything,*' were her last words to me."

"Maybe she was right" remarked Greg.

Annie and Greg were due to return to Australia. Annie felt washed up. Spending their last days in Dublin, they drove into the Mountains where she once again became overwhelmed with sadness. "What if I don't get on the plane?" she said.

"What are you saying?" Greg snapped, in frustration. "Why would you want to stay in a place where they have it all stitched up? I wanted to confront them, but you wouldn't let me."

"It's because I didn't want a scene. I didn't want my mother upset."

"Well, honey! If she was my mother I'd be taking her right away from them."

"Jesus Greg, I'm stuck between a rock and a hard place. I ask myself, did I do as much as I could for her, and can I live with myself if I abandon her and return to Australia? I never really did stand up to Theresa. I was always worried about how it might affect mam. It's all fucked up." Greg put his arm around her.

"You must do what you need to do honey. I will help you either way."

"Thanks Greg, I appreciate your support."

Because of separate flight arrangements, Greg would leave Ireland from Dublin and Annie from Shannon. The plan was that they would meet in London and fly to Sydney together.

Annie asked Anthony if it would be OK to leave the Katemobile on his property. This arrangement was fine.

Annie didn't get on the plane: Panic, remorse, the pain of separation, her promise to Kate, and the fact that Joan Mc Hugh had left her post, Margaret O'Callaghan never went to see Kate as she had promised; all the disappointments, knocks, and setbacks had reduced Annie to a physical and emotional wreck. 'There has to be another way,' she kept telling herself.

The travel agent sounded sympathetic but explained her flight cancelation came with a cost. "I don't care, I need to stay." She drove Greg to Dublin airport and waved him off. She had another panic attack. 'What's happening to me?' she asked herself. People all around were floating, their lips were moving, but she couldn't hear their words. She found herself driving around the countryside. She loved the countryside but the 'black dog' was at her side.

When she arrived back in Limerick, Anthony shook his head. "What happened?" he asked.

"I couldn't walk away," she said.

"It will never be any different Annie; can't you see that? Theresa will never release her grip. She will never let go. She's the controller, the head of the family and no one on earth will change her mind. You can't reason with someone who is unreasonable. We are wasting our energy, and that woman will cause me to have another heart attack. Enough is enough Annie." The tears ran down her cheeks.

"I hear you Anthony," she said, "but I'm still finding it hard to leave. I made a vow that I would come home and look after mam. Fuck! I'm so mixed up. I'm grateful to you and Pam for allowing me to stay with you. Without you, I would have broken long ago. It's my decision to go back to Ballyfermot and see if anything changes."

"Whatever you feel you need to do Annie, but I really think you should have gone back with Greg. You should have gone home."

"Where is my home Anthony. I don't know where home is."

Lying awake that night she was not sure of anything, not her marriage, her family, not even her reason for staying in Ireland; her self-doubt consumed her.

Greg phoned. He had arrived in Australia and was on his way to the farm in the country. Annie had always enjoyed the drive over the Blue Mountains, to reach their country retreat.

The next day she told Anthony and Pam of her plan to return to Ballyfermot, and maybe try again. The following weekend after packing up her belongings she returned to Spiddal Road. Mr and Mrs Dunne were friendly and hospitable to her, and once again she apologised to them for the state of the back garden. Greg and she had tried, but without the proper equipment their efforts were futile. She suggested to the Dunne's, that if they contacted the Dublin Corporation, they might clear the garden, as a health hazard.

As she waited those long days to see Kate, she tried to occupy herself with housework. She would do anything, as long as it didn't involve spending money.

Looking up from the front of the day-care centre, she saw Kate standing near a second floor window. How sad, she thought, that she wasn't free to take her for a drive.

She had made her way inside, and as soon as Kate spotted her, she immediately lit up with excitement. "Oh my God! It's you, it's you Annie. Dear God, thank you so much for sending her to me. Annie, oh Annie, I am so happy." Kate was weeping, her bottom lip quivered as melancholic tears flowed down her face. Annie had never witnessed her mother so down like this. They hugged. Kate put her hands on Annie's face, "You're such a beautiful girl. You are my lovely Annie." Annie felt her heart was going to burst. They sat on the sofa and held hands. "Annie you always made me happy. When you were a little girl, you brought me so much happiness." On feeling Kate's love, Annie realised that no matter how they tried to poison her mind, the love that Kate had for her was as strong as ever. The bitter-sweetness of the moment hit her profoundly.

She decided to wait in the car park until the bus came for Kate. She had figured that it would be less upsetting that way, but she was wrong. Kate did her best to convince the bus driver that she was going with Annie. "Mam, I'm sorry I can't take you today. It will have to be arranged. How about, I arrange a little trip too Mayo. Greg and I stayed in a hotel there, and it's very cheap, but beautiful. Would you like that?"

"Of course, Annie. We would be together."

"Yes mam. Now go on into the bus and I'll see what I can arrange."

"I love you Annie."

"I know mam, and I love you very much." As the bus pulled away Kate's hand was on the window.

They never did go on the trip to Mayo. And that was to be the last time Annie would see her mother, before going back to Australia

Annie sent a text message to Theresa, *next Monday I would like to take mam on a short holiday to Mayo for four days?* The reply was immediate, *it does not suit!* 'It does not suit... It does not suit!' Annie repeated these words over and over to herself. Jesus! Why is she doing this?

That night Annie began to accept that Theresa would never change. She Skyped Anthony. He tried to reassure her, by telling her that Theresa had got what she wanted, she'd won, and her trophy was Kate. It was not that she wanted to be with Kate, she just didn't want Annie to be with her. When Annie hung up from Anthony, she started to panic; an incredible fear loomed over her and for a while she felt chest pains and thought she might die. She couldn't understand what she was experiencing. The night that followed was long and somewhat restless. When morning arrived, she was in a state of confusion, about what direction to take. She decided to ride the bus into Dublin, and while on the bus she sent a text message to Cathy's sister, Nuala. '*Am heading into town if you happen to be around for a coffee?*'

Chapter Twenty

Nuala had business in town and arranged to meet her at 'Bewleys' later in the morning. Annie wasn't sure of her original reason for going into Dublin. The previous night she had toyed with the idea of abandoning her reason, hence leaving Kate. Seeing her, not seeing her, had become too painful for both herself and Kate. In the early part of the morning Annie walk the streets in a stupor. She found herself inside the travel agents. The girl asked, "How can I help you?" There was a lump in Annie's throat and her eyes filled with tears as she struggled to say, "I must leave. I'm broken. She's won. My mother is lost to me." The young woman stared at Annie, with both curiosity and sympathy. Annie had sat with this girl a few weeks earlier while making enquiries about airfares, to take Kate to Australia.

"I am so sorry," said Annie, as she composed herself and allowed the girl to arrange a flight for ten days time. This gave her time for goodbyes.

Still somewhat distraught, Annie left the travel agents and had begun walking toward O'Connell Street. Feeling faint, she leant against a store window and began weeping. Passers bye looked on in bewilderment. She gathered herself and continued to walk. Returning to Australia was a huge decision, but she must stay determined and stick to it. Speaking with Kate the previous day had been both lovely and painful. The memory of her loving words would stay with her forever. She decided she would not say goodbye to Kate. She would simply walk away.

Inside a shop she was looking through a Celtic calendar when her phone rang. She placed the calendar on the counter while eyeing to the assistant her intent to buy it. "How are you Annie?" asked Pam. "Anthony told me what happened with Theresa. Are you ok?"

"I'm a mess. I've booked my flight for the end of next week. I don't want to leave, but I have no choice. I'm beat." With that

Annie began to weep. The shop assistant stood awkward at not knowing what to do. "Pam, I will ring you later." Annie hung up.

"Can I get you some water?" the assistant asked.

"I need a hug, I just need a hug" said Annie. With that the assistant came from behind the counter and hugged her warmly and in a way that allowed Annie to express her complete sadness.

After thanking the assistant, she made her way across the city. It was nearing her time to meet Nuala. Her mind was filled with Kate and her heart was still heavy. Nuala was standing outside the cafe waiting and immediately recognised that all was not well. Over coffee, they discussed Annie's return to Australia. Nuala agreed it was for the best. During their conversation, Annie spoke of the loose ends she needed to tidy up; one being a visit to the head quarters of Alzheimer's Ireland, in Blackrock. "That's near where I live," said Nuala. "If you come to Dunlaoire by bus, I'll take you to Blackrock."

"Thank you," Annie replied. "I'd love to walk on the pier one more time. Is tomorrow OK?"

"Tomorrow will be grand," agreed Nuala.

After they parted, Annie stood on Grafton Street, not knowing whether to turn right or left. She remembered a mental note that she'd made of an expo on the Life of W. B. Yeats' that was being held at the National library. 'Perhaps I'll find some peace there,' she told herself.

As she entered the display hall, some of her spirit returned. A voice could be heard reciting the poem, *The Swans at Coole*. An amphitheatre of sorts had been set up using two large screens on either side of a larger screen. The words of the current poem were being displayed on the central screen and the two side screens were displaying images of swans on a lake.

Annie allowed her senses to indulge in the sounds and imagery of Yeats's life and his poetry. The continuous audio visual display went through many of his poems, before starting over again. Annie lost herself, in pleasure, as the appropriate image matched the poem. While there, she looked at several of Yeats handwritten poems, some showing his mistakes, changes of words, and his scribbled notes and corrections. She looked at his glasses, his clothing, his photos, and other items that would have been precious to him. She left the expo feeling richer for her connection with his poetry.

She rang Pam on Skype and filled her in on the date of her flight. Warm friendly faces filled her screen. She told Anthony of her decision not to see Kate. "If I go back, I'll die," she said, and added, "It's more than I can bear."

"It's OK Annie. In your last memory of mam, she is telling you her true feelings. Nobody badgered her. She was not influenced by Theresa to deny you. Annie, I'm also tiring of the battle. Let her have her trophy. Let her find out what it's like to look after mam, as her condition worsens. You're right to go back to Australia. You need your family. You need to simply walk away from this."

"I feel I'm abandoning her. It could have been so different."

"But it's not," he reaffirmed. "And don't think it will ever be anything other than what it is. Theresa has successfully wrecked the family. She believes that she's the head of the family. She's not. What she is is the head of no family. You have nothing to reproach yourself about Annie. The simple truth is, you tried with all your heart, but you were stopped. Pack up your bags and spend the last few days with us. The kids would love that, and so would we."

"I'd like that. I need to go to Dunlaoire tomorrow. After that I will head down."

"We'll have your dinner in the pot waiting."

Annie caught the 46a to Dunlaoire. The weather was ordinary but she didn't care. She had fond memories of Dunlaoire. When she and Damien were courting this was one of their favourite places. On arriving at her destination, she caught sight of the pier and smiled. Nuala and herself buttoned their coats and headed for a brisk walk along the pier wall. She felt happy that she had made the trip. Nuala was a lovely girl. They walked and talked, and little by little, Annie's spirit lifted.

Later they were joined by Nuala's husband and the three of them drove to Blackrock and the Office of Alzheimer's Ireland, where Annie thanked and waved them goodbye.

She had brought a bracelet to the office of Alzheimer's Ireland. This particular bracelet is worn by Alzheimer's sufferers in Australia. She had phoned the Irish office before leaving Australia, explaining how these bracelets were not just for basic identification. They also had a number that the police could use to access all kinds of information, including, the name, and address of the wearer, medical records, family doctor, etc. Such a scheme did not exist in Ireland. The receptionist made a phone call and then directed Annie to wait in an adjoining room. A manager came and spoke with her and during a short but interesting meeting, Annie handed the manager one of the bracelets from Australia. She regretted not contacting them earlier, as she found everyone there so helpful and friendly. The conversation between Annie and the manager somehow came around to Kate's situation, and how easy it was, to gain another person's pension, by getting a signature from the vulnerable Alzheimer sufferer. The manager agreed that this should be looked at by the Dept of Social Welfare. Annie thanked the manager for her time.

After returning to Ballyfermot and packing her bags Annie headed for Limerick. She had selected some up-beat music to distract her thoughts. She felt that she had left Ballyfermot forever. The drive seemed to pass quickly and by late afternoon she had arrived in Limerick. Anthony hugged her warmly and after eating a meal of bacon and cabbage, they began re-capping the events of the last seven months. Annie spoke of the things she'd never achieved, including, not taking Grace and Sean to Dublin. "You can still do that," said Anthony. "You have nearly a week. The children would love it."

"Brilliant!" she said. "I'd like to show them the Ardagh chalice, and take them around the museums."

That would be so wonderful."

And so it happened, that the following day Annie and the children went to Dublin, where Brenda had kindly let them stay with her. They bought tickets for the tour bus that travels the sites around the city. They hopped on and off all day. The bus driver told Annie, that for some reason the bus company was extending the use of the tickets for a second day, at no extra charge. These proved to be two of the most enjoyable days she would spend with her niece and nephew. Sean had the bus passengers in hysterics with his antics. Annie realised that he had the same sense of humour as her son Daithi. She took them to see the Yeats expo. This delighted Grace, who remarked that her teacher was a Yeats nut, and they, the students, were currently learning the poet's early masterpiece, 'The Song of Wandering Aengus'. Annie bought Grace some literature and bookmarks to give to her teacher.

When they arrived at the National Museum, they were disappointed that the room, housing the Ardagh Chalice, was closed, due to flood damage. However, seeing the 'Bog Men' proved so interesting, that it made up for their earlier disappointment.

At the newly opened Leprechaun museum, a story teller had been relating to the crowd, the legend of Balor of the one eye. "Legend has it, "she said, "that Balor can flip his eyelid up, and put an almighty curse on the poor unfortunate that looks into his eye." With this, Sean did his party piece. He folded both eyelids upward to expose his eyeballs. The crowd, including the story teller, were in stitches.

From there they went to the wax museum and Christchurch Cathedral. Next was St Michans Church, where Sean point blank refused to go into the crypts. Neither God nor money could persuade him. They all enjoyed Kilmainham Jail and Phoenix Park, where the bus driver allowed them to hop off to buy an ice-cream.

In two days they had been to more places than they had thought possible. They had a meal in the 'Bad Ass Cafe,' simply because Sean loved the name. They posed in front of all the famous statues around the city. Finally after two fantastic days of memories, they headed back to Limerick.

Anthony took Annie for a drink in the local, where a surprising turnout of people congregated to wish her a fond farewell. As usual, after singing the night away, they left the pub in the 'small hours'. That last night/morning, Anthony and Annie stood in the kitchen and had their last supper of Tayto's on bread and butter.

"I'm going to miss you Bro," she said.

"Me too," said Anthony. She raised her mug of tea.

"A toast," she said. "To mam."

"To mam."

Over breakfast on the morning of her departure she discussed the possibility of coming home to live. Her goal was to buy a cottage in the west. It was a school day for Grace and Sean. Annie hugged them warmly and thanked them for sharing so much fun and joy with her. They all cried a little and the children said that they were going to miss her terribly. With her cases packed into the boot of the Katemobile, she said her last sad goodbye to Pam. Pam had reassured her that Kate would be fine, and that they would get up to visit her, in the care centre, as often as possible.

Annie's drive to Shannon airport took nearly an hour. Sitting in the passenger seat she watched the outlying towns and villages whizzing by. She felt she had come to know the streets and back alleys in her time spent here. Speaking, with a somewhat false merriment, Anthony tried hard to be upbeat, as he drove towards their big goodbye. Annie removed the beads and crucifix that Kate had hung from the mirror and placed them safely in her handbag.

An exceptionally quick check-in at Shannon airport had left them standing in an awkward silence. "Just go," Annie said, with the words forming a lump in her throat.

"I'm fine."

Just go Anthony, It's really ok." They hugged and without a word being spoken, they began to cry. Anthony turned and walked away while Annie watched until he had reached the exit doors, where he looked back and gave a sad wave.

As the plane taxied down the runway Annie felt her heart had been left behind.

Not wanting to make small talk with other passengers, she put on a set of earphones and her mind drifted back to her childhood: Oliver swaying in the room. Anthony singing to the litter of puppy dogs. She remembered the other children on Spiddal Road, how they would all hang out together in the evenings; sitting on the railings or swinging from the lamp post. Oliver was strict on Annie coming in at seven prompt. He would stand at the front door and call out to her. This behaviour would embarrass her. She constructed feeble excuses to leave the group early before he got the chance to show her up. The other kids all seemed to have lenient parents.

She recalled her first kiss at twelve. It was with a boy from across the road. Back then the kids called there first kiss, 'the ware.' When one young lad told her that 'Donal' wanted to give her 'the ware,' she was flattered. She felt she wasn't as pretty as the other girls, and was pleasantly surprised to get this invite.

The evening it happened she was ecstatic. Afterwards she kept touching her lips and going over it in her mind. She took to counting each time Donal gave her a kiss. It was 'first love' and it felt great. One day, Oliver came home from work early to find her *first love*, behind the hall door with his arms around her. Oliver went mental. Donal took off across the street, after vowing to Annie that he would wait for her forever. Oliver said that if he ever caught anyone inside the house again, all hell would break loose. Kate spoke with Annie, telling her that she was not allowed to have a boyfriend until she was sixteen. Annie agreed and told Donal that perhaps he should find another friend. They would both look out their windows at night and wave goodnight to each other. Annie now smiled as she pondered these memories. She was so innocent back then.

Kate got herself a job in the Cafeteria at Woolworth's. It caused a commotion in the house that night. She got ridiculed by Oliver for not staying home with the children. He detested the fact that she had found herself a job. It hurt his pride. She had been finding it hard to make ends meet. Oliver was drinking heavy and only gave her forty pounds housekeeping money to last the week. When they got home from school there would be food left out for them, usually a large pot of rice.

Annie's memories of Theresa were a bit vague. Theresa is two years older, so at that time, she was given a little more freedom. She stayed up longer, got the top bunk, stayed out later. While baby-sitting her siblings, she always acted like she was the big boss. 'You go to bed. You dry the dishes. You, get out of that chair.' Quiet often Annie and her brothers would just laugh and walk away. A particular evening is etched in Annie's memory: Theresa became so livid at their lack of obedience that she feigned to faint on the floor. Annie and the boys fell about laughing. Theresa got so embarrassed that she jumped up and stormed off. This made them laugh even louder.

More memories came into her head. In later years while Theresa was showing off a new attic conversation, Annie asked her, "Why all the Indian dream catchers, and ornaments?"

"Because we are Indian," she replied. Annie looked at her in amazement, and said,

"Our great-great grandfather married a lady from India, not America. She worked for the British Raj. Sorry Theresa but you have the wrong Indians." Annie wondered how Theresa could have been so mistaken. Didn't she revel in all the interesting family history, or did her imagination take her to different lands? "Hiawatha" Annie muttered, while smiling.

Annie began piecing together events that stood out in her

memory. What was Theresa's problem? There was an instance where Kate, while sitting on the sofa next to Annie, reached over, and in an awkward manner, tapped her shoulder, "Annie," she said. "It's so nice to have you here with me. I'm so happy you're sitting beside me." Later, while in the kitchen, Annie related the scene to Theresa "It was so cute how she tapped me and said that," remarked Annie. With that Theresa responded with abhorrence. Shouting with such venom that spittle sprayed from her mouth. "SHE – NEVER - DOES – THAT - FOR ME…"

"That's because she see's you all the time. I live in Australia. I'm the *'prodigal,'* that's all that it is."

The more Annie pieced things together, the more she wondered if jealously was behind Theresa's behaviour.

Amidst the drone of the Jet engines, older and equally bad memories began to surface: Annie was a girl again and the household on Spiddal Road had become tense. The television had taken over the lounge room and Kate had started going out socially with a lady friend from work. 'Mary Poppins' was Kate's nickname at the store where she worked. With a soft humour and her kindly nature, Kate proved popular amongst her colleagues. A co-worker named Angie had befriended her and the two women went out together occasionally. Angie had separated, a few years earlier, from an abusive husband and the relationship between herself and Kate had proved both happy and convenient for both women.

For years, Oliver had kept Kate under his tight control. The pittance of 40 Pounds a week housekeeping money, had meant that Kate's energy was spent on making ends meet. With her new job came financial independence. Oliver found this new *status quo* hard to live with. Kate had for many years been happy to stay at home looking after him and their children; in fact, she had spoken with Oliver about adopting another child. Oliver, it seemed, had been in agreement with her. Due to a spinal injury acquired after

Anthony's birth, there became no question of Kate enduring another pregnancy. They contacted the same adoption agency that had arranged Thomas's adoption. They were offered two small brothers, and Kate was elated with the idea. The paper work had progressed to where it needed to be signed. It was at this point Oliver pulled the plug on the whole thing. Kate was devastated, and subsequently fell into depression. Her regard for Oliver changed. And from that day, things in the house would never be the same. Because of Kate's depression, the doctor recommended, something to occupy her mind, suggesting outside employment might be the tonic.

"Where are you going?" Oliver asked, as Kate put on her overcoat.

"I'm going to the Irish club with Angie." She kept her nerve as she straightened herself in the wall mirror. The children felt the tension. Oliver's head looked like it was going to burst as he struggled to find the words to answer her. It was as though his tongue had been killed by indignation. He looked to the television, and then back too Kate. With little to-do and without making any eye contact, she calmly put on her gloves and neck-scarf, picked up her handbag and left the house. Oliver turned off the television and sat back down. His fingers began drumming out his agitation on the arm of the chair, his teeth clenched and his head swivelled from left to right, the veins in his neck had inflated to bursting point and his pursed lips were contorting as he sucked and blew like a mad bull through his flaring nostrils. The children sat speechless; terrified to cast even the tiniest corner of an eye in his direction. He stood up from the armchair, scurried over to the front window and peeked out to the pavement. He then opened the front door and called back to Theresa,

"Look after them," meaning the children, and then he left the house.

He looked up and down Spiddal Road, but there was no sign of Kate. After figuring she must have caught a waiting bus he walked at double pace straight to Downes public house, where he ordered a pint of Smithicks and a chaser. The barman knew his tipple by heart.

"Most of boys are at the match," the barman offered, as Oliver scanned the few faces left scattered around the bar. For the next ten minutes, he continued to seethe. He was jealous of her, yet he couldn't see it. She was loved by everyone who had met her. For years Oliver consoled himself in the delusion, that she was his property. He was belligerent and had few, if any friends. He took solace in his ability to maintain control over his family. He felt that Kate's new found independence was a complete rejection of him. He could only think in terms of obligations and rights; he had rights, and Kate had obligations. He caught sight of the bus, through the pub window, and hurried out the door.

While he was continuing his journey, Kate and Angie were sitting in the snug of a city bar. With stain glass windows, red velvet upholstered seats and a crackling open fire, the atmosphere in the bar was exotic to. Kate. She would only take a drink on special occasions, and tonight she had indulged in a snowball, (a cocktail, made up of advocaat liqueur, with lemonade and a squeeze of lime). "You're looking especially beautiful," remarked Angie, as the two women stood to leave for the Irish Club.

"Ah thanks Angie." Sure, now that we're out of our woollies uniforms, don't we both look gorgeous?"

A while later, Oliver alighted from the bus at the city terminus and begun his walk towards the Irish Club. On entering the club, he scanned the revellers until he spotted Kate and Angie. They had, only seconds before his arrival, seated themselves at a table close to the stage. Kate was laughing at something Angie had said, and in turn, Angie laughed herself. As he pushed and shoved his way towards them, the joyful scene incensed him. When he appeared beside them, they stopped laughing and looked at him dumbfounded. "You," he said, in a loud aggressive voice, while pointing to Kate. "are neither a good wife nor a good mother. Look at yourself? You're dressed up like a whore. You're a cold frigid fish, with no warmth whatsoever for your husband." Kate shrivelled in the face of his rant; she wanted to vanish. She prayed that he would stop. She felt as though the entire world was looking at her. Angie stood.

"I'm sorry Kate. I should go. This kind of behaviour is why I left my husband. I can't listen to this. I'm so sorry." Oliver then turned his attention to her, accusing her of encouraging 'his wife' to behave like a whore.

"If it weren't for Woolworths and people like you," he said, "she'd be at home in her kitchen." Distraught, Angie put on her coat and left.

Kate felt numb, as she walked behind him down along O'Connell Street. She had always been a gentle person and tonight she had battled her emotions, only to become overwhelmed with hopelessness.

On other occasions when Oliver lost his temper he threw Kate and the children out of the house. Annie remembers a night where she held hands with her brothers, and with Kate by their side, they walked towards the city. As they walked aimlessly, she sang a song to try and buoy her sibling's spirits. Annie couldn't remember why they walked in that direction, or how it resolved, but she remembered that Kate would refuse to worry her own parents with this problem. Her parents also lived in Ballyfermot.

A lifetime of thoughts swirled inside Annie's head. She remembered Kate talking of her trips to a nursing home in Cork Street. She would buy a packet of cigarette's to share with the men, and a packet of jelly sweets to share with the ladies."

"Don't you think that sexist," Annie had joked.

"No, not at all," she responded. "Those two small packets, I would share with nearly fifty people."

In the later years, Annie was thinking how her mum had become quiet religious. She had acquired fame around Ballyfermot and Thomas Street, and was known as, the 'Lady with the Petals." To Kate, the petals were precious. She would say that when held to the light, they showed images of the Blessed Virgin and Christ. She believed in the petals so much that it became contagious. Word spread that 'Kate's petals' could heal the sick. She received phone calls from people who desperately wanted their loved ones cured. She frequented the Dublin hospitals, where she brought hope to the sick, and comfort to the dying. She would sit in a grotto for hours, while people flocked around her. The thought of it put tears in Annie eyes.

Chapter Twenty One

On Annie's arrival at Sydney airport, Greg was waiting with a bunch of flowers. The gesture, though appreciated, did little to touch her spirit. In the car park he pointed to the shiny new Falcon, "This is yours," he said, and her heart sank. Seven years of worry, was all she could see in his gesture. Life should have been getting easier. She had turned fifty and the debts appeared insurmountable. She didn't feel like she was home. The landscape that whizzed past her window now appeared foreign.

The forty five minute drive from Sydney airport, took her to where Greg and his sister had rented a house in her absence. Once inside the house, Greg pointed to the large flat screen television. "That's yours as well," he said, "It's your birthday present." Annie snapped.

"Don't bullshit me Greg. And don't insult my intelligence. It's not my present. You bought it for yourself."

"Ah well," he let go, "I may as well tell you the rest. I spent another five and a half grand on the Harley paint job. Annie just walked away.

She spent the next few days trying to avoid any thoughts of her future. She withdrew to her bedroom, where she tried to relive her last scene with Kate. The memory evoked a paradox of a beautiful melancholy. She held Kate's beads and crucifix and prayed, 'please God, keep me safe, please God, keep me safe.' She didn't have the strength to play happy families, and she had begun craving her own space.

Returning to work became both a distraction and a pain. She was constantly asked how her trip went, but with each explanation she felt the sorrow consuming her. She longed to go completely insane to be able to let go of all her frustrations, disappointments, and anger.

She found herself at the doctors for a routine check-up. "Welcome back," he said. "I thought you were staying in Ireland?"

She unfurled the chronology of events. The doctor listened intently and sympathetically, before replying, "That's terrible, both, for your mother, and for yourself. I have heard similar stories here in Australia. One patient told me that he had received a phone call one morning informing him that his mother was dying in Brisbane. He was advised to get there as soon as possible. Four hours later he was met by a nurse in the corridor, offering condolences, while also explaining that his mother had died at 10am. She was not alone, the nurse had said, your brother was with her. The man was grateful for this information and with sadness he left the hospital. A day or two later, the family discovered that their mother had died at 10:00 am. And at 10:15 her savings account had been cleared out from the ATM at the hospital."

"That is wicked," said Annie.

"Annie, perhaps you need to talk about what has happened. Do you think you might need counselling?"

"Sometimes I do," she replied. "I had several panic attacks while in Ireland. I think the pressure has affected me emotionally, I don't know what to think; maybe I just need to get angry?"

"I'll give you a referral. There is a lady who works out of this surgery. She has a good reputation. Give her a call when you're ready."

Annie had, to some small degree, got back in the swing. She currently worked just the one part time job. Before leaving Australia she had another job with a government agency. They had agreed for her to take six months leave and when she didn't make their timeline, they advised her to resign. It wasn't all bad as she now had time to catch up on old friendships.

The family farm in the country was the perfect place, for Annie and a couple of girl friends, to get away from it all. Things did begin to look up, and she was starting to feel like her old self again.

During one of these trips she received a phone call. "Hi," said the voice, "my name is Tina. We met last year. You came to care for Elizabeth, my mother. I was just wondering if you would consider taking care of her, from Monday to Friday, in her own home. As you are both from Ballyfermot, It would be so good for her. Since she had her stroke, she hasn't left the house. I would love to give her back some quality of life, and within reason, you can name your price. My legal work in Sydney leaves me little time to spend with her. What do you think?" Annie was caught by surprise and asked for time to think it over. "That's fine," said Tina, "ring me when you decide."

Annie was finding, the sharing with her in-laws, somewhat difficult. Although they were lovely people, they enjoyed watching TV in the evenings, whereas, Annie longed for quiet. Most nights she would withdraw to her bedroom and put the ear phones on. Sharing the house became an increasing struggle, and with no rational reason to complain, she became more and more depressed. After deliberating Tina's job offer, she arranged a time to meet her and discuss the details. She also called the day care centre in Ireland and asked if she could speak with Kate. While waiting, she could hear the carer asking Kate to sit down and take the call. "Hi mum, it's me Annie."

"Hello sweetheart, it's so nice to hear your voice. Are you coming to collect me?"

"Sorry mum, I'm in Australia. But hopefully I will get there soon."

"That will be nice Annie. You are my girl. I pray for you and your family, every night."

"I know you do mam. I love you very much, and don't you ever forget that." Annie heard Kate speak to someone.

"She said she loves me."

Annie's began taking care of Elizabeth. She took her on outings and accompanied her to social occasions. Previously, Elizabeth had spent her days alone at home. Annie was at Elizabeth's house, when her phone vibrated. It was a text from Liam in Ireland. *"Hi, cuz, just to let you know that 'Fat chops'*

(Liam's slang name for Theresa), is telling family members that you came back to Ireland to rob your mother's assets, and that she had to protect Kate's money, from you."

Annie's jaw dropped, and she felt sick. This revelation shook her and she began to berate herself for not doing more to stop Theresa. 'I must be weak,' she told herself, 'and because of me, my extended family are now having to suffer Theresa's lies.' Slipping back into depression, she began to get sick, tired, and was finding it hard to sleep. She lost all sense of normal smell and taste. Certain food types had a strong taste of ammonia and would make her spit her food out. Shampoo and others products, smelt of ammonia. Her doctor sent her for several tests, including a brain scan. They all came back negative. The doctor concluded that her problem's was due to stress.

Chapter Twenty Two

Christmas was nearing, and she made a special effort to pick herself up. Again, she felt grateful for the distraction of work. One week after Christmas she received a text from Anthony, '*When you are free, Skype me.*'

"Hi Anthony, happy New Year. How are you?"

"Hi, Sis. I have something I want to tell you. We decided not to say anything earlier, as we didn't want to spoil your Christmas.

"What is it?" she asked. There followed an anxious few seconds before he replied,

"Theresa and Adrian have applied to the courts for Enduring Power of Attorney over mam. It seems they had taken her, along with Mrs McGee and Betty, to a solicitor to sign the relevant paperwork." Anthony took a breath before continuing. "Now here comes the interesting part: They did it on the fourteenth of July of last year, just after they found out you were coming home, then they waited a year and a half before lodging the paperwork. That date was the 21st December just gone. Fortunately, the Judge smelt a rat and asked Theresa's solicitor if Kate had any other living children? When informed that there were three other children, he directed Theresa's solicitor to inform all of her children. So Annie! I'm guessing your letter is on the way. We will have 28 days to voice our objections.

"The bastards!" Annie cursed, with a mixture of anger and conviction. "Mrs fucking McGee, and Betty. What hero's they must think themselves, to have witnessed our mother signing such important documents; and we were told nothing. No decent doctor could have assessed mammy as Compos Mentis."

"But Annie, it was signed by her doctor

"Well, then," replied Annie, "the doctor had no idea or didn't care what she signed. If Theresa is successful, she will have complete power over mammy, including, who she may or may not associate with; she could stop us from seeing our own mother, the house the pension, everything would be under Theresa's control."

"We will object Annie. There's not a judge in the land that would grant them this power."

After ending their conversation, Annie began to pace the floor. She felt uneasy and scared that she might never see her mother again. Long into the night she re-lived Theresa's plotting and deception. She relived Adrian roaring at her. 'You are not taking your mother from this house. She does not want to see you.' Annie remembered the words they put in Kate's mouth 'I'm not going with you, Theresa is good to me, and she gives me my dinners.' Once again Annie was in tears.

Tina was still in the kitchen when Annie arrived for work

"Are you running late?" Annie asked.

"I'm going straight to court, so I don't have to leave as early."

"I need legal advice," said Annie, and proceeded to share Anthony's revelation.

"You should appoint a solicitor in Ireland," she suggested. "If they have a solicitor, you get a solicitor, if they have a barrister, you get a barrister. You will need to match their fight." Annie was grateful for the advice, and decided to find representation in Ireland. She sent Anthony a message, telling him of her intensions. Later she received a reply from Anthony's wife Pam, saying it was putting them under yet more pressure to expect them to pay for a solicitor. Annie read on and was shocked with the tone of her message. Annie didn't care if she paid for the cost of the solicitor. The family needed professional help and she wasn't going to leave anything to chance. She had never expected Anthony to pay. She was trying to be diplomatic and not embarrass him but her intension had been misread. She apologised to Pam for the misunderstanding, and made it clear that she was determined to appoint a solicitor herself. She rang five solicitors in Ballyfermot and they all declined, citing the fact that she lived in Australia. However, after persevering, she was successful on her sixth attempt. Philomena was the solicitor's name, and she was Annie's only hope.

Annie had taken to spending more and more time at the farm, where she threw herself into reading, writing, and reflecting on life. Time appeared to stand still. Greg arrived in the kitchen one day, after chopping wood, and while switching the kettle on, he asked, "What's the latest with the solicitor?"

"She's taking the paper-work into the Four Courts on Monday morning," Annie answered. "I'd love to see Theresa's face, when she finds out that I'm objecting."

"Will the solicitor ring, or email you?"

"Actually. I said that I would ring her."

After Greg had retired for the night, Annie stared into the flames of the fire. She had no idea how it would all turn out, yet, she felt positive that standing up for Kate was the right thing to do. It was different when she was in Ireland; there she had to stay quiet so as not to upset Kate. But that was then, she told herself, and this is now.

That night Annie slept in front of the fire. After waking with the sun she stoked the embers of the fire and fed their flame.

She phoned Ireland. "Hi Philomena. It's Annie. How did it go?"

"It was very interesting," she replied. "Your sister appeared surprised to see me there. In fact, I think she was a little put out. I lodged an objection on your behalf and was granted an adjournment for one month. During this time we will have to work hard at gathering the information needed to make our case."

"I'm sure that won't be a problem," said Annie. "Philomena, I want to thank you so much. I was worried that I might miss this window of opportunity."

"It's good that you nipped this in the bud Annie. I will contact you in a day or two, and fix a date, for an in-depth interview." Annie felt good after their conversation.

Later that week she had lunch with her daughter, Lisa. "I don't know why you didn't just knock Theresa to the ground," said Lisa.

"I would have done.

"That's not my way," Annie responded. "And I hope I never stoop to such a level. I have never, in all the time I spent with your nanny, uttered one bad word to her about Theresa. Your Nanny Kate is a sick woman, and the last thing she needs, is behaviour like that. I left Ireland believing I didn't have a voice. But it seems I've been given a second chance. I'm going to tell it, as it was. I don't need to embellish anything. I'll simply tell the truth." Lisa had listened intently.

"I guess, you're right, but I'd still love to knock her over."

Philomena finally called back, and she asked all manner of questions. She wanted to understand the family's dynamics: She asked about Kate's relationship with Oliver, about Kate's education and general intellect, she asked how Annie's siblings grew up and how each turned out. Philomena appeared to be building a picture of Kate, before and during the Alzheimer's. "It will take a while to write it up," she said. "We must state our case, as to why Theresa should not be granted Enduring Power of Attorney. Are you aware Annie, what these powers entail?"

"I have a limited knowledge," she admitted.

"If granted," she explained. "Theresa could sell Kate's house and she could say who Kate associates with. There are many reasons why we should fight this Annie. I still have a lot of work to do. If I need to, I will call you again."

Annie felt happy that things were happening. Yet, the possibility of failure remained a cloud. She remembered something her father had drilled into her as a child. 'Sweetheart,' he had said, 'the only thing that matters in this life, is your integrity. One day you may find yourself in a fight to the death for your integrity.' Annie drew strength from his words.

Annie contacted Anthony to discuss how he might be able to help Philomena. "I'll dig out the file number for the ombudsman," he said, "as well as the email I sent to Theresa. It predates their application, for Power of Attorney. It should help to explain our objection."

The next two weeks proved anxious for Annie. She told Philomena about the biscuit tin full of receipts that was secure in the civic centre. She also asked the elder abuse officer to contact Philomena with anything that might help Kate. Annie's phone rang. "It's Philomena. We have a few hurdles."

"And they are?" asked Annie.

"Firstly, Doctor O'Connor states, that your mother was in good mental condition when she signed the paperwork."

"Philomena," replied Annie. "I'm a dementia specific nurse. I know my mother. In 2001 she was diagnosed with Alzheimer's disease. She didn't know what day of the week it was. Eight years later in 2009 she was worse. I returned to Dublin in 2008 to find her living in squalor. She was so far gone; she didn't know how to ask for help. Her toilet was broke and she didn't understand to call a plumber. We found several thousand Euros squirreled away in her bed, and when questioned, she didn't understand the concept of money. That was one year before the doctor signed a document saying she was well. Alzheimer's sufferers progressively get worse not better. I put it to you Philomena, that if my mother showed signs of improvement, then doctor O'Connor should have taken a blood sample. Perhaps Kate is carrying the *cure* that the world is searching for. What I believe Philomena is, the doctor signed a form based on what she had been told by Kate's carer, namely Theresa. I believe Theresa had a hidden agenda and misled the doctor. The doctor told me, that she believed, my mother had been living with Theresa for two years at this point. I know for a fact that was untrue," concluded Annie. Philomena made no comment and moved directly on to her second point.

"Theresa's solicitor has also stated that Kate appeared perfectly fine on the day she signed." Annie paused before responding…

"All I can say is, they took Kate to their solicitor, who was a stranger to Kate, a fact that in itself appears suspicious. The same solicitor was working on their behalf, and that has to be a complete conflict of interest."

"Annie," continued Philomena. "It appears that Kate wrote an affidavit; in it she states, that she foresaw your return from Australia and that you were going to cause trouble. She also stated that she did not want anyone other than Theresa to control her affairs, specifying that she does not want Annie, Anthony, or Thomas to interfere with these wishes. It also states that she wants to appoint Theresa's mother- in-law as her witness."

"Oh my God Philomena. In a thousand years I would not believe, not even for one second, that my mother said this. Someone else wrote those words and got her to sign it. May God forgive them?"

"One last thing," added Philomena. "Theresa claims to have a letter, written by your father on the day before he died. She claims the letter specifically states his wish that his eldest daughter Theresa should take total charge of all Kate's affairs."

"Really Philomena, did she put words into her dying father's mouth? I was at his bedside the day before he died. He had been in a coma since the Monday and he died on the Thursday. If by some miracle he managed to write such a thing it would not have been worth the paper it was written on. My understanding of Enduring PA is that you, yourself appoint such a person, not your husband, from his deathbed."

"That's correct Annie. Thank you for all that information. You have a good handle on this. I believe you. Still, we will have to watch everything."

After Annie hung up she felt sick in her stomach. She had the image of her mum, sobbing as she held her face: '*You are my lovely girl*' '*I want to be with you, I want to be where you live.*'

"Bastards, bastards…" Annie repeated to herself

Anthony appeared amused at the idea of Oliver's death-bed letter to Theresa. He scribed a parody of its contents and emailed it to Annie.

'Dear Daughter,

When I'm gone you'll be the new head of the family! I would strongly recommend a dictatorial style of leadership as it has always served me perfectly! And don't forget to demand respect - It's the least you should expect from them.

Anyway I want you to take care of your mother who has Alzheimer's.

So here are my instructions;

1. What the experts say about Alzheimer's is all wrong so when you're mother starts to say things that are untrue remember she is telling you lies and must be punished!

2. When her personal hygiene begins to deteriorate remember the "pen and ink" is only being fabricated by her to make your life a misery and embarrass you! So if you notice that her surroundings are falling apart the best thing to do is ignore her.

3. Don't check her requirement for heat and proper plumbing as this will only encourage her!

4. If you notice rancid mould infected dinners on dining room tables just leave them there as the evil bitch is just trying to test you!

5. Should she then have the opportunity to be properly cared for in her own home where her life is the central issue do all in your power to stop this shit! Actually use intimidation - it worked for me!

6. Any vermin nests which may appear in her home were probably put there by her in order to "do your fucking head in!" And remember she'll never need curtains!

7. I always found the best way to deal with your mother was with plenty of aggression! Try to control everything about her - Especially what she thinks!

8. I know there are two brothers and a sister involved here, but always remember that they don't matter! You're the head of the family now! Your opinion and wishes are the only things that

*matter. Lie, cheat, and steal whatever it takes! Remember the
Godfather - Don't be an honest pushover! Shoot the punks!
9. it's far better to be the head of a broken family than just an
ordinary member of an ordinary family! Whatever it takes to be
"The Head" do it. Even if that includes the total destruction of any
kind of order! Even if it is detrimental in the end to you mothers.
Quality of life - that's not what's important here. Take it from me; I
know what I'm talking about! It's all about you! Everything! About
you and your standing! Your mother's relationship with her other
children? Don't make me laugh! Remember if you don't control it
then it's not worth considering.
10. Remember "Truth" is whatever you say it is! I even convinced
my psychiatrist of this! So whatever they are saying is always
wrong and you are always right!*

*So daughter these are my instructions which over-ride just about
any moral decency that I can think of. And now when the world
stops revolving around me it can begin to revolve around you! So
yes, when you feel like a victim you're right, it's all their fault.
And one final tip - Always remember "they" are watching you! So
if you are leaving the house don't leave in a bunch! Split up and
confuse the punks!
Your Loving Da.'*

Annie rang Philomena for another update. "We had to file for
adjournment," said Philomena. "We are still preparing documents
and gathering evidence. Your sister's solicitors have been far from
helpful. In fact they are downright rude. They told me that your
sister was angry about our request for an adjournment. I asked
them to forward the power of attorney documents. They sent me
one part, knowing full well that I needed all five. They sent me the
one your mother had signed. It's obvious they are playing games.
Their conduct is unprofessional. Anyhow, much to your sister's
disgust, we were given another month."

"Ah well! That's how it goes," said Annie. Theresa did tell me that I would never be able to do anything. Thank you Philomena. Talk soon."

Annie was remembering the hurt bestowed on herself by Theresa, yet, she now felt a *nothingness* towards her. Annie questioned herself as to how she could feel neither love nor hate. She summed it up as a numb feeling. She felt *numb* towards her sister.

Other than her new preoccupation of worrying about the upcoming court case, the next month passed without remark or incident. She knew in her heart that she had conveyed everything to Philomena, and that the outcome was now in the lap of the God's.'

Annie had lapsed from the Catholic teachings. Although, she still believed that a *higher power* existed and that higher power would come to her aid when she most needed help. She felt comfortable with the relationship she had developed with this *God of her understanding*. She would find herself talking to him; even thought she didn't believe her God was male or a female. Sometimes she would have humorous conversations with her God, even though the replies were never instant.

Years prior, an event took place that Annie believed was the most profound showing that her God had ever made to her. The pressure of the recent separation from her husband Damien was immense. Kate, prior to the onset of her Alzheimer's, had asked for Annie and the children to come back to Ireland for Christmas. During this time Annie's family and friends had also tried to convince her to remain in Ireland. While this would have suited her personally, she felt that she could never take the children from their dad, and for that reason they all returned to Australia. However, on returning to Australia, the dilemma remained, and she still didn't know if she should go or stay. After speaking with a councillor about her fears, she had begun her journey home. On passing the local school grounds, she recognised her son Daithi in the playing field. "Is something wrong?" she called out to him.

"I've lost the compass from my watch," he said, as he held out his arm to show the place where the compass had fallen from. The compass was about the size of a thumbnail. She felt sad for his loss and went to his aid.

"Where were you playing?" she asked. He waved his arm, indicating a huge area of ground. "Let's separate," she suggested. "That way we might have a better chance of finding it." She never really believed it possible to find such a tiny thing in the area the size of a soccer field, but she wanted to show him that she was trying. After looking for a while she stopped. "Ok God, I need help?" she asked, tongue in cheek. "As you must know God, the child has recently lost his dog, and on top of that his parents are separating. So, give the lad a break?" Annie looked down and there in front of her shoe was the compass. "Thank you, thank you, so much God." Daithi ran to her side, and she picked him up and swung him around. 'Daithi, you need to say a thank you.

The following morning at 5:00 am, Annie sat upright in bed and exclaimed aloud, "Dear God, a compass! I nearly missed the sign. The compass was not about Daithi, it was a sign for me. I had lost my direction, and you were sending me a sign."

Chapter Twenty Three

The court date had arrived, and Annie was on her way to join Greg at the farm. A job opportunity presented itself, which Greg had accepted. He needed to live at the farm to be nearer this workplace. When Annie arrived, in the afternoon, Greg had the fire blazing and they enjoyed a nice meal together. They went for a stroll down by the creek. With the time difference, Ireland was still sleeping. The evening at the farm seemed to drag on forever. Greg went to bed early and Annie sat staring into the flames. She tried to occupy herself with a book but she couldn't concentrate.

She had earlier asked Philomena how she thought the decision might fall. Philomena said that she didn't believe Theresa would be awarded Enduring Power of Attorney. She felt, with all the evidence that was presented against her, the judge would be cautious about granting Theresa such power. The judge may suggest that Kate be made a 'ward of the court'. However, it was not in his power to make this happen, but he could make a recommendation to that effect. If this were to happen, then it would be a completely different ballgame.

Midnight came and went and Annie began to pace the floor. At around 1.30 am she sent Philomena a text, *'Hi Philomena, any word yet?'* Annie stared at her phone and almost immediately it vibrated, her heart pounded and her hands shook, as she pressed the button to view the response.

'WE WON... I will talk tomorrow. I have so much to tell you.' Annie, fell to her knees. "Thank you God, thank you so very much." She sent a text, *'Have the best day Philomena. Thank you, thank you.'*

Annie chose not to wake Greg. She felt vindicated. She felt giddy, but most of all, she felt an absolute relief that Kate's welfare had been taken out of the hands of Theresa and Adrian. She rang the local florist in Ballyfermot, which was situated only three doors from Philomena's office. *"Philomena loves white flowers"* suggested the florist.

"White flowers it is," said Annie.

'*Would you like to write her a message?*

'*Yes, write, 'thank you so much Philomena for giving us back our mother. Anthony, Kate, and Annie."*

"That's wonderful," said Greg, on waking to the news. "I don't have details as yet," said Annie, "but Philomena said she would speak with me today. Oh thank God. I feel so relieved Greg."

Annie spent the rest of that day pottering around the farm. She walked into the knee high grass in the lower paddock and spun herself around, in giddy childlike excitement. She flashed back to her childhood days, where life was the size of her housing estate. She had long since discovered the big wide world, with all its big world wonders, but she would never forget her roots, on the contrary, she was extremely proud of her earthy beginnings.

Later that evening she rang Philomena. *"Hello Annie. Thank you so much for the flowers. They are exquisite. It's very nice to hear your voice. There is much to tell,"* continued Philomena. *"As you were texting me yesterday. I was standing with our barrister on the steps of The Four Courts. This is Annie, I said, showing him my phone screen. He smiled. I have to tell you Annie, this has ended up being a very significant case indeed. I am so proud. There is a possibility that laws may be changed in Ireland due to what your sister almost got away with. The judge was so annoyed with Theresa that he stated that he would seek a meeting with the President of the High Court of Ireland to discuss this very case. Theresa's solicitor was visibly shaking when he heard the judge say this. Theresa looked so angry. The Barrister saw her and whispered in my ear, 'look at the way she is staring at you, I am expecting any second now a red dot to appear on your forehead"*
. *I think I saw Thomas in court,"* Philomena commented. *"Do you think Thomas would have been there to support her?"*

"I really don't think he would," Annie replied. *"He never had*

a kind word for her and he felt that Adrian was an arrogant bastard. Besides which, if he hates our mother like he stated, why on earth would he be there. I don't understand. I really don't think it was him."

"Annie, this fellow was a tall handsome sort of fellow. I really believe it was Thomas."

"I have no idea Philomena, but I am so relieved that Theresa was not appointed Enduring Power of Attorney."

"It was important that she did not get that power," Agreed Philomena. *"You may never have seen your mother again if she had."* Annie's blood ran cold with the thought of it.

"I swear to God that would never happen," said Annie, *"I would have walked away from my life in Australia and come home. I would have chained myself to the railings of the Four Courts until someone listened to me. As God is my judge Philomena that would not have been the end of the story, it would have been the beginning of another."*

"Annie, I must thank you also for your role in protecting your mother. Not many people, when push comes to shove, are prepared to go to the lengths that you did. I commend you Annie."

"Thanks Philomena. What now?"

"It is now the Court v Theresa. I will keep you informed."

Annie and Greg had celebrated with dinner in the nearby town. Shortly after returning to the farm, Annie received an email from her brother Thomas. She began to feel sickly as she read.

'Hi, I must congratulate you. Wow! Well done! Pat yourself on the back. Not a lot of children have the balls to take their MOTHER to court. Fair play to you, you have done it and you have won. So congratulations again just in case I forget. But what have you won? Your vendetta against Theresa? Don't think so... If anything you just made her a lot stronger mentally. She won't thank you for it, so I will... THANKS. Anyway that's all the nice things out of the way so let's get down to the MURRAY saga. While I have done my fair share of talking behind backs which we all have I'm sure

*that's what family's do. Of all the bad things I done in my life I
don't think and I hope I never will stoop to your level. I keep
asking myself why you went to so much trouble to stop your
Mother being cared for. Surely you can't hate your sister that
much. So sad. And then I ask where you were for the past 20 odd
years where was Anthony, I certainly wasn't there I was happily
living in Cork. 2001 Dad died we all turned up for the funeral and
then we all went home. So who picked up the pieces? I certainly
didn't and I can only speak for myself. If you stayed for years after,
well fair play to you. Well contrary to what you might think, inside
your ever increasing evil mind. Theresa really did look after our
mother OK so what if she didn't have her 7 days a week. Big
fucking deal. Where the fuck were you where the fuck was Anthony.
I certainly wasn't there I was happily living in Cork. Yes it is great
MAM being look after, nothing to worry about, the arrangement is
fabulous. Bring MAM down every once in a while, go to Dublin
every once in a while, what more could you ask for and it suited all
of us living in Ireland. So what change everything? Well I guess
you have it in your mind Theresa is only looking after MAM for the
money.*

*O yes! Adrian is out of work let's get MAM to move in so we can
rob her money. You really are sick in the head how you could even
think that. I really can't understand if you even bothered to ask
about MAMS finances you would have seen all but no, head first,
straight for the juggler run to the Garda report to social services
what the fuck is all that about. It's just so sad that anybody could
stoop to that level. I tried to stay neutral in this fiasco but you did
say to me I need to take a side so I have MAMS side. I am not
writing this to defend Theresa I am sure she can do that herself but
she is caring for MAM so I guess I am on her side to. As you know
I hate MAM so it must be guilt and ye I had my issue with dad
but who didn't but they were my issue and I am dealing with them.
You also asked me would I comfort you God forbid if something
happened to Daithi my answer NO. You and in your words, your*

puppet have managed to split this not so close family. You know it might not have been so bad if it was kept between our family but to post it all over the web really is in the gutter. So I guess that's all I have to say don't bother replying I am not really interested.'

"Oh my God! Greg. Why did he write such a nasty letter?" It then dawned on Annie that Philomena was probably right. He may have been in court alongside Theresa. "He doesn't want a reply? Oh my God."

"You can't let him get away with that," said Greg. "It's a totally distorted view of what happened. You didn't bring your mother to court, they did. You didn't involve the Garda, they did. Don't take this shite Annie."

Annie felt a huge sense of loss and betrayal. She replied to Thomas matter of factly, while trying to keep her emotions out of it. Thomas never replied.

For the next few days she went over his email. She showed it to Anthony, and asked his opinion. He remarked, that with the language used and its presentation, he felt that Thomas may have been under the influence of alcohol and was just having a rant. This did not give Annie much solace. She was broken hearted. The following week she spoke with Philomena about Thomas's email. They agreed that Thomas most likely attended court, at Theresa's side. Philomena spoke of a meeting between the judge and the President of The High court of Ireland. It had been decided to call in the big guns and another meeting was set up between these parties and the Solicitor General, "Wow!" said Annie.

"Indeed," replied Philomena. "This is big-time stuff. Again as soon as I know anything I will tell you Annie."
"Thanks, talk soon."

Annie once again felt a sense of justification for her actions. Informing her work colleagues of the latest update, several of them encouraged her to write about these events.

The next several days went by without much happening,

during which time Annie busied herself with work, grandchildren, and life in general. When she next spoke to Philomena, a decision had been made as to Kate's legal future. "After many discussions," said Philomena, "It has been decided, that Kate will be made a Ward of the State. Theresa was denied her application for an Enduring PA. A committee, which does not include Theresa, will be appointed by the government,. This committee will make all relevant decisions concerning Kate's health and welfare. Kate's assets are to be frozen. Theresa will not have access to Kate's finances. Kate will still be permitted to live with Theresa. When and if, Kate needs to go into a nursing home, the committee will make that decision. Theresa will not be happy. However, I feel it's for the best. My colleagues also, are very pleased and suggest that these findings may be written up in the gazette."

"You did a great job Philomena," said Annie. "The next time I'm in Dublin may I call on you?"

"I would love to meet you in person." said Philomena. "I admire the courage you have shown. One final thing Annie, I doubt very much if you would get it, but would you like me to draft a letter of demand to relevant office of the courts, requesting that Theresa pays you your costs?"

"I never thought about it," said Annie, "I hadn't thought about anything other that justice for our mother, but yes, go for it."

Annie felt comfortable that Kate was in the hands of the government. She rang Anthony at his home in Limerick and informed him. He too was over the moon with this news. "What a thought! Think about it Annie? We will never, have to ask Theresa her permission to see our mother," he continued. "Can you just imagine her in court? The steam must have been coming out of her ears. We have disempowered her, and that has to be a good thing. Well done, Annie!"

Chapter Twenty Four

Annie tried to take up the threads of her life, but what should have been a sweet victory, had left her feeling more and more depressed. It felt to her like she was suffering 'post traumatic stress syndrome.' On a visit to her doctor, she explained how she felt. "You've been through the mill," he said. "I think you should talk with the lady that I spoke of. I've been told she's excellent and her costs are covered under Medicare. You have nothing to lose in speaking with her."

"I feel like I need to admit that I am struggling," said Annie. "I feel worn out. It's like I was living on adrenaline, and as the court case was looming I had to keep going, but now that it is over and I should be feeling triumphant, I actually feel like I have smashed into a brick wall. I think the timing is right to seek help in making sense of it all."

Life for Annie had become something of an anticlimax. It was like Ireland had gone silent. Kate was at day-care five days a week. Annie would ring her weekly. Anthony had written to Kate's *case officer* stating his intentions to take Kate for some family time in Limerick. He asked the case worker if she would arrange for Theresa to have Kate's medication and clothing sent with her to day-care on a certain date. He would pick Kate up from this neutral ground, and return her the following week.

Kate had a great time in Limerick, and was treated like a queen. Annie went onto Skype and got to see her in person.

Several months had passed when Annie took a random notion to check her laptop for, *'house's for sale'* in Ireland. Her eye's nearly popped out of her head when she saw Kate's house was on the market. The added photo's showed that it had been totally cleared of its former contents. Every stick of furniture, even the new curtains were gone. Annie was shocked. She immediately sent Anthony a message, telling him what she had discovered. Anthony sent Kate's case worker an email, asking why the house was on the market, and who made this decision and why the family were not informed. Later that day he received a reply stating that it was the court's decision to sell, and that they were not obliged to discuss the details with all members of the family. However, they did invite Theresa to bring Kate to the house to collect personal belongings. Annie was saddened by this news. It was final, her dream was dead. She could never bring Kate home to Spiddal Road again. Kate had lost so much. The only solace Annie could salvage was that Kate would never know the impact of what had happened. 'The wall of memories?' Annie wrote to the case worker asking what had happened to the photos. The old photos had been Kate's connection to her family. What of all the old toy's that were stored in the attic? Why weren't other family members asked if they wanted to collect such items? It was their family home, after all.

The following year Annie went home. She arranged to pick up Kate, with the intention of bringing her to Limerick. This was pre arranged through the Four Courts. The entire situation saddened Annie. However, the Courts ensured access to Kate. Annie would not have to ask Theresa, and be denied this basic of human rights. All that was now in the past.

When Annie arrived at the day care centre, Kate was over the moon to see her. They took another road trip and had the best time. Kate's condition had deteriorated so much that Anthony and Annie took her to the doctor: Her knees were full of fluid. Walking was difficult and painful and her breathing was laboured. On checking her over, the doctor believed that her heart was out of rhythm. Her memory had deteriorated to where she believed Anthony was Annie's son. "No mum, he is your son," explained Annie, as her eyes welled with tears.

Annie returned with Kate to the day-care centre. Kate had been spoilt with presents from her family in Limerick. Annie stayed with her until the mini bus was ready for the drop off. While they stood in the car park, Annie took the opportunity to get Kate's belongings from the boot of her car. When she arrived back the driver had already loaded all the clients onto the bus and Kate had been jammed into a seat behind the driver's seat. "I haven't hugged her yet," said Annie.

"Jump in there onto my seat," said the driver, "you should reach her from there." This last hug was awkward and incredibly sad for both women. And as Annie watched the bus drive Kate away, it was like all the pain she had ever felt suddenly came flooding back.

She drove to Ballyfermot where she bought the biggest bunch of white flowers and took them, three doors up, to the office of Solicitor Philomena Best. While a young girl enquired as to Annie's business, an older woman was talking on the phone. Annie recognised the older woman's voice. "Would that be Philomena over there?" she asked. The young girl looked at Annie.

"It is," she said. "May I ask your name?"

"Actually, I would like to surprise her. If that's ok?'

Annie's face to face meeting was very welcoming and big hugs were easily given. Annie sat in Philomena's office for some time while discussing the entire affair. Philomena told Annie that the case was very significant. "While they did not change the law after this case," she said, "they made huge amendments to it. It's now much more stringent to apply for Power of Attorney. The paperwork is carefully checked out, and all persons concerned must be blood relatives of the 'Donor." Annie then asked if it were possible to be privy to the affidavits from the case. "Sure," said Philomena, "I will have my secretary prepare them for tomorrow." The two women hugged, and in high spirits, Annie left the office.

She went to visit Mr and Mr Dunne, and was told what had occurred in regards of the house being sold: A young lady arrived one day at Kate's house and when asked, she told the Dunne's that she worked for a solicitor from Dublin. She had been given the task of clearing out Kate's home. She did this by hiring a skip, and with the help of two men, all Kate's belongings, her memories, and her life were effectively, dumped into a skip, and removed.

In Annie's imagery, the bare Christmas tree, that had once held pride of place, was thrown on the top of the skip. Annie wanted to weep for the lack of respect shown to her mother. She clearly remembered Kate's words, '*This is my home, and these are my things.*' As Annie was leaving the Dunne's, the young man, who had bought Kate's house, struck up conversation with her. Annie explained that this had been her family home until recently. He invited her to see the renovations. On stepping inside, her eyes opened wide. There was nothing that reminded her of her home. All the walls had been knocked down, leaving the entire downstairs, an open plan. It was tastefully done out in a contemporary style. "There were *french-doors*, hanging there," she said, pointing to the spot.

"I took them down," he replied. "There they are outside." Annie felt sad that Kate never got to enjoy her beautiful doors. Upstairs, the bathroom and toilet were now in one room, including a brand new WC and shower recess. Kate's old bedroom was a storage room for the moment. Annie's old bedroom felt different. The ghost's had finally gone. She thanked the young man, and wished him every happiness in his new home. Their time was done on Spiddal Road.

On the long haul flight back to Australia, Annie took the Affidavits from the overhead luggage compartment. She sat for hours reading through the paperwork. She felt both sad and angry when she saw her mother's signature's on documents that she knew in her heart were achieved by trickery.

'I have instructed my solicitor Pauline Harahan that I nominate my daughter Theresa McGee as my power of attorney. I nominate my son in-law's mother, namely Fran McGee and also a friend of my daughter namely Betty Parrington, whom I know very well of my intention. I do not want to notify my other children Anthony,

Thomas, or Annie that I am creating an enduring power of attorney, as I believe they will interfere with decisions in relation to my health, property, and finances. My daughter Theresa has looked after me for the last eight years and also looked after her father for many years before he passed away.

I have a very good relationship with my daughter Theresa. I trust her to look after my decisions in relation to my health and all my financial affairs'.

Whilst reading, Annie was twirling the ring on her finger. She became conscious of this and began to stare intently at it. A strong image popped into her head.

It was Christmas 1992. She was back home in Ireland with her children, for the Christmas period, when Kate took her to one side. "Annie," she said, "this is really important to me." She then placed two rings into Annie's palm, one was her engagement ring from Oliver, and the other was an emerald dress ring. She closed Annie's hand firmly around them, saying, "I want you to have these rings. Do not tell your sister. I want you to have them.

"Are you sure?" Annie asked, with some surprise.

"Yes," came her simple reply.

As the airliner droned it's long monotonous single note, Annie put her head back onto the seat and closed her eyes, and with a sad smile and tears welling in her eyes, she recalled Kate's last words to her: 'You are my lovely girl Annie. You have always made me happy'.

The End

Made in the USA
Charleston, SC
23 August 2014